Moms *Like* Christ

Supermom

Sarah L. Bibler

This book is a work of non-fiction. Unless otherwise noted, the author and the publisher make no explicit guarantees as to the accuracy of the information contained in this book and in some cases, names of people and places have been altered to protect their privacy.

WestBow Press books may be ordered through booksellers or by contacting:

WestBow Press
A Division of Thomas Nelson & Zondervan
1663 Liberty Drive
Bloomington, IN 47403
www.westbowpress.com
1 (866) 928-1240

Interior Image Credit: Kaytlin Bibler Photography

ISBN: 978-1-9736-8905-8 (sc)
ISBN: 978-1-9736-8906-5 (e)

Library of Congress Control Number: 2020905455

Print information available on the last page.

WestBow Press rev. date: 03/26/2020

Dedication

I would like to dedicate this book to my loving, patient, and compassionate husband, Curt. You have inspired me to continue when all I wanted to do was quit. You lead me with Christ at the center of our marriage and friendship. Your love for God energizes me to follow in your footsteps. I love you forever and always.

Contents

Preface

Dear Mommas,

I am so proud of you for taking some time for you. As moms we put ourselves last on the list of priorities. Our families' needs always take precedence over what we need for ourselves. Well, today you have taken the steps to do something for you. I wrote this book series with two purposes in mind: 1. To help women (moms) draw closer to God, and 2. To create an environment where the older women can mentor the younger women. This journey will not be an easy one. Satan does not want either of my intentions to be successful. He will encourage you to quit, make you feel inadequate, remind you of all your failures, and make the journey seem impossible. Don't let him win! Together we can make it through. Believe in yourself, even if it's for the first time in your life. Stay at it! Start today! You're worth it! Your family is worth it! God is worth it!

Acknowledgments

> Older women likewise are to be reverent in behavior, not slanderers or slaves to much wine. They are to teach what is good, and so train the young women to love their husbands and children, to be self-controlled, pure, working at home, kind, and submissive to their own husbands, that the word of God may not be reviled.
> —Titus 2:3–5 (ESV)

First, I want to thank God for using me as His vessel in writing this book. For many years I have journaled, noted, and jotted information down, and now it has been brought to completion. All praise and glory belong directly to my Lord and Savior. He directed my path and helped me to become the woman I am today. It is God who will make this book useful to the women who pick it up and diligently study it. Thank you for always guiding and leading me, Father.

Next, I want to thank my family for their patience and help as I made this book series a reality. Thanks for helping with all the housework, leaving me alone so I could focus, encouraging me to keep at it and not give up, and for loving me even when I fail. To Curt, you are the man of my dreams, and I love you forever and always. Thank you for loving me right where I am and pushing me to fulfill my dreams. Thank you for being my best friend. Thank you for being a wonderful father to our children. To Kaytlin, thanks for sharing the laptop with me. Thanks for not getting upset at me when I pry into your life. Thank you for being one of my best friends. I love you always, my sunshine. To Noah, thanks for asking me about my book and helping take care of Opal, our cute little puppy. All those trips to take Opal outside and 'oopsie' pickups don't go unnoticed. To Caleb, thank you for staying up late with me while I was typing or writing. You always asked me about my book and now you can say your mom is an author! Thanks for encouraging me all the way through.

Next, I need to thank a lot of people that helped develop me into the woman I am today. My parents, Mike and Donna Porter. My brothers, Andrew, Ben, Daniel, and Isaac. Sorry for all the times I beat you up and told Mom you were the guilty one. To my sister, Anna Turner, for taking the leap of faith to become an author so I would know what to do. To my best friends for life, Katrina Groce, Annette Troyer, and Amber Grant. You ladies have inspired me more than you will ever know. Your unconditional love, helping talk through frustrating times, letting me cry on your shoulder, and leading me to God's Word not only have helped me, they have helped my family survive.

Thank you to Jenn Hemlinger, Amber Grant, and Katrina Groce for proofreading and showing me love all the way through this journey.

I would also like to thank both sets of grandparents, Don and Janet Peters and Nolan and Wilma Porter. You each created the spiritual inheritance that helped build my foundation in the right spot. I miss you, and I'm looking forward to worshiping together in heaven one day.

Teacher Leader Guide

First of all, thank you! Stepping up and leading a women's Bible study is not an easy task. I appreciate your time and effort (emotionally, mentally, physically, and spiritually). God will bless you for your efforts. No doubt in my mind!

How long do I need to set up my weekly meetings?

How many women should be in my group?

- ✓ 5–7 women = 1-hour class time (on average). We all know how a group of women can talk, talk, talk …
- ✓ 8–10 women = 1½-hour class time
- ✓ 10 or more = 2-hour class time

How long is this class designed to take?

- Week 1 is an introduction to the book series. Read through the introduction, it's about a Relationship, Make a Commitment, and Mapping God's Word.
- Each additional week should cover one chapter in the book (weeks 2–13). Spend the week reading the chapter. Discuss the end-of-chapter review at your next meeting.
- Optional week (14) to just get together to celebrate all you have gained through this study.

Basics of Leading a Women's Bible Study

Use these steps to prepare yourself to lead this group of women:

1. **Be prepared for anything**. While writing this book, God has shown me there will be women who go through this Bible study who are experiencing struggles. Please be respectful of their privacy.
   a. **Do not force women to share if they do not feel comfortable sharing**. This will only increase their anxiety and disappointment in themselves.
   b. **Be respectful of time**. Women are giving their time to meet with you. Please keep the classes moving along. Now, don't move so fast that women feel they cannot share their hearts. If a lesson takes two weeks instead of one, so be it. As long as the extra time is useful. Useful means uplifting women and drawing them closer to Jesus. Use your discernment. God will let you know when to push on and when to just sit and listen.
      i. If you find a woman in your class is taking up a lot of time that takes away from other women being able to share, talk to her one-on-one. Sometimes these women just need someone to listen. Be that ear and express your concern, in love, to them.
      ii. If at any time conflict arises between any women (including yourself or any participants), sit down with the women involved and talk through the struggle. Seek assistance from an elder's wife or pastor in extreme situations when you need help to make peace.
2. **Lead by example.** Each week have your lessons finished to the best of your ability, memorize your verses, share your testimony (seasons of your life that apply to the lessons in the book), and whatever God leads you to share.

3. **Be an encourager to all women**. You will have women from all walks of life, all levels of spirituality, and all emotional status. Don't expect everyone to be the same. Only speak to uplift and never tell a woman she is doing it wrong. Maybe you can make suggestions, but don't be too pushy. We want the women in your Bible study to feel safe with their surroundings. It's God's job to make us feel uncomfortable when we are not reaching up to His potential for our lives. Let the Holy Spirit weed out those that need motivating. God works in mysterious ways. Don't get in His way. Let Him lead.
4. **Bring snacks**. We women—well, probably men too and children—love to eat! You can make it healthy or not. Coffee, hot cocoa, or tea are great too.

Procedures to follow when leading this book

First meeting with your group:

1. "Get to know you" activity
   a. Find an activity that will fit the group of ladies you will be meeting with. Share names, number of kids, hobbies, funny stories, whatever works. This will help break the ice to get your group talking together.
2. Read through the introduction of this book and the It's about a Relationship section.
   a. Emphasize the importance of keeping everything discussed together private. Otherwise, you will not gain as much as you could with these women.
   a. Let the women know that if there are struggles, they need to come and talk to you about them.
   a. A relationship with Jesus Christ is by far the most important part of this journey.
3. Read and sign the Make a Commitment pledge
4. Go through the Mapping God's Word example briefly. Encourage your group to refer back to this section for their weekly quiet times.
5. Explain weekly procedures:
   a. Each week is set up by five days per chapter: Days 1, 2, 3, and 4 plus the review day.
      i. All materials on these pages need to be completed before the following meeting time.

ii. The review page at the end of each week will be used for discussion at your weekly meetings.

Weekly meetings:

1. Weeks 1, 3, 5, 7, 9, and 11:
   a. Review chosen memory verses. Partner up and practice reciting memory verses. Each week recite all the memory verses you have from previous *Moms Like Christ* studies plus this book.
   b. Discuss the review questions as a class. Allow women to share their responses, but do not force anyone to speak.
   c. Each woman should share one verse she mapped this week. (This is the part that will take the majority of your class time).
      i. Share each section of their verse map.
2. Weeks 2, 4, 6, 8, 10 and 12:
   a. Review memory verses from previous weeks. The more repetition, the longer you will remember the verses.
   b. Discuss the four questions from that week's Bible character study day 5 review page.
      i. Allow women to express their findings, even if they are different from your own. You may find something new that someone else discovered.
      ii. I have included summaries of each Bible character in this book. These summaries may have information you wish to share with your group. Use them as you see fit.

Let's keep in contact

I would love for you to contact me and let me know how things are going. I would love to chat or answer any questions you may have. I can share your stories on the book's Facebook page. I want to support you in any I can. I definitely want to pray for you. So seek me out!

My contact information:

Email: csbibler@mail.com
Website: momslikechrist.squarespace.com
Facebook page: Moms Like Christ

*This is a public page. You are more than welcome to follow me and post pictures or comments about the progress of your class. Do not post any personal information of any woman in your group. You can invite them to my page, and they can post any personal information for themselves. I would love to see pictures of your group of ladies! That will help me when I'm praying for your class. I can put faces to the groups out there.

Participants Guide

First of all, thank you! Stepping up and participating in a women's Bible study. I appreciate your time and effort (emotionally, mentally, physically, and spiritually). God will bless you for your efforts. No doubt in my mind!

How long do I need to schedule for weekly meetings?

- ✓ 5–7 women = 1-hour class time (on average). We all know how a group of women can talk, talk, talk …
- ✓ 8–10 women = 1½-hour class time
- ✓ 10 or more = 2-hour class time

How long is this class designed to take?

- Week 1 is an introduction to the book series. Read through the introduction, it's about a Relationship, Make a Commitment, and Mapping God's Word.
- Each additional week should cover one chapter in the book (weeks 2–13). Spend the week reading the chapter. Discuss the end-of-chapter review at your next meeting.
- Optional week (14) to just get together to celebrate all you have gained through this study.

Procedures to complete this bible study

First meeting with your group:

1. "Get to know you" activity
2. Read through the introduction of this book and the It's about a Relationship section.
    a. Emphasize the importance of keeping everything discussed together private. Otherwise, you will not gain as much as you could.
    b. If you experience any struggles with the content or other women in your group, please talk to your group leader.
    c. A relationship with Jesus Christ is by far the most important part of this journey.
        i. Read and sign the Make a Commitment pledge
        ii. Go through the Mapping God's Word example briefly. Encourage your group to refer back to this section for their weekly quiet times.
        iii. Explain weekly procedures:
    d. Each week is set up by five days per chapter: Days 1, 2, 3, and 4 plus the review day.
        i. All materials on these pages need to be completed before the following meeting time.
        ii. The review page at the end of each week will be used for discussion at your weekly meetings.

Weekly meetings:

1. Weeks 1, 3, 5, 7, 9, and 11:
    a. Review chosen memory verses. Partner up and practice reciting memory verses. Each week recite all the memory verses you have from previous *Moms Like Christ* studies plus this book.
    b. Discuss the review questions as a class. You are free to share or you may refrain from sharing. Keep in mind we learn from each other by life experiences. Your story may bring peace, hope, joy, or more to another woman.
    c. Share one verse you mapped this week.

2. Weeks 2, 4, 6, 8, 10, and 12:
   a. Review memory verses from previous weeks. The more repetition, the longer you will remember the verses.
   b. Discuss the four questions from that week's Bible character study (day 5 review page).

Let's keep in contact

I would love for you to contact me and let me know how things are going. I would love to chat or answer any questions you may have. I can share your stories on the book's Facebook page. I want to support you in any I can. I definitely want to pray for you. So seek me out!

My contact information:

Email: csbibler@mail.com
Website: momslikechrist.squarespace.com
Facebook page: Moms Like Christ
*This is a public page. You are more than welcome to follow me and post pictures or comments about the progress of your class. Do not post any personal information of any woman in your group. You can invite them to my page, and they can post any personal information for themselves. I would love to see pictures of your group of ladies! That will help me when I'm praying for your class. I can put faces to the groups out there.

Introduction

The job of being a Christian mother is very intense and overwhelming. She must not only see to the physical needs of her children, she must stay aware of the psychological, social, and spiritual needs of each child. While being alert to all these conditions, she must keep the house clean, complete tons of laundry, satisfy her husband's needs, maintain a social life of her own, and keep her sanity. Moreover, some energetic mothers have a job outside of the home. Feeling overwhelmed yet? Me too!

When we become mothers, our children are a blessing from God.

> "Children are a heritage from the Lord, offspring a reward from him." Psalm 127:3 (NIV)

We, along with our husbands, are called to raise our children according to God's Word.

> "Start a child off in the way he should go, and even when they are old they will not depart from it." Proverbs 22:6 (NIV)

> "Fathers, do not exasperate your children; instead bring, them up in the training and instruction of the Lord." Ephesians 6:4 (NIV)

As we run the race set out before us, we will encounter God in so many different aspects of our life. God reveals Himself in and around us as long as we continue to watch for Him. We will hear stories from our parents, grandparents, and great-grandparents. Many of these stories may include revelation of God working in the lives of our ancestors. We should cherish these stories. These are what I call faith builders—experiences we use to increase our faith and trust in God.

God calls the older women to help lead the younger women (Titus 2:3–5). We older women have experienced many different seasons of motherhood. Through each season, we struggle to make daily decisions that will help equip our children for life in this ever darkening world. As young women, open your hearts and ears to the older women God has placed in your life. As older women, pray and seek God's will for using your stories to help encourage and uplift others.

Every story in the Bible leads us to a deeper understanding of who God made us to be. As mothers, we search His Word to discover the best ways to raise our children. God has so graciously given us guidelines, but how do we draw the connections between motherhood and His Word? That's what this book is all about: taking God's Word and the lessons therein and applying them to our lives. Join me on this journey as we study God's Word. We will focus on fourteen traits of a mother after God's own heart:

Book 1: A Merry Heart

Massive prayer life
Order to chaos
Merry heart
Sacrificial love

Book 2: Emotional Wreck

Loves unconditionally
Insight into our children's lives
Keeps the faith
Emotional wreck

Book 3: Super Mom

Contentment
Holds true to God's Word
Release children to God
Inspired by others
Super mom
Trust in God

As we study each of these attribute, we will relate it to different women from the Bible. Some of our examples are true godly women who lived their lives to please God. Others are women who knew of God but never took the time to draw close to Him. We can learn from each of these types of women. Every word in the Bible is for our growth as Christians. Join me on this adventure—you won't regret it.

It's about a relationship,
not about a religion.

Before starting into this book, I have an extremely important question to ask you: "Do you have a relationship with Jesus Christ, or do you have religion with Jesus Christ?" Some of you may ask, what's the difference? Aren't they the same thing? Well, I'm here to inform you they are very different from each other.

When driving through any town or city in America, you see different denominations of churches: Methodist, Catholic, Church of God, Church of the Brethren, Mennonite, Lutheran, and more. There are even churches that claim to be nondenominational. What does denomination actually mean?

*Denomination: a religious organization whose congregations are united in their adherence to its beliefs and practices.[1]

Basically, denominations of churches have their own religious acts that govern their beliefs about God. Let's relate it to something most of us are familiar with—food. I prefer tacos myself, so let's start there. One denomination may say that the members of their congregation may choose to use hard or soft taco shells. Another denomination may choose only soft shells. While another denomination may use only whole wheat soft shells. You see, each denomination has created rules and/or regulations for their members based on human understandings of the scriptures. Some denominations base their beliefs and/or regulations off of more than just God's Word. They use other writings to govern their members actions. Denominations set up the way the church will run or be run by those who are a part of its churches. This is what makes up Christian religions in the world. Religions are dictated by the opinions of their leaders or developers (men and women).

*Religion: a personal set or institutionalized system of religious attitudes, beliefs, and practices.[2]

Religion is based on a human's interpretation of God's Word, which sets the boundaries and rules for those who live out its belief.

*Relationship: the state of being connected.[3]

A relationship is actually a real connection. We all have relationships with those we call family and friends. Some of our relationships are wonderful. Wonderful relationships bring happiness, joy, love, support, peace, and tranquility to those involved. The connection of these individuals is strong and healthy. Other relationships are destructive. Destructive relationships bring sorrow, pain, hurt, unruliness, and discomfort. Unfortunately, we all may have destructive relationships in our lives too.

I want to ask you my original question again: "Do you have a relationship with Jesus Christ, or do you have religion with Jesus Christ?" If you have a religion with Jesus Christ, you have rituals you follow that are based on your church and/or beliefs. I am not saying that your religion is wrong. As long as it is based solely on God's Word, you are doing exactly what God would want you to do. If your rules or regulations are not found in God's Word, then your religion is void. It is a waste of your time to perform. God calls us to live like Jesus Christ, His Son. Either way, whether your religion follow's God's Word or not, it is simply religion.

God calls us to have a relationship with Him; a connection between us and Him. Have you asked Jesus into your heart? If you have, you should have experienced a change in your life. When we begin a relationship with Jesus, others see a change in our life as a reflection of Him. If you have not experienced a change in your life, then you have not truly begun a relationship with Him.

If you want to gain anything from this book, you must have a true life-changing relationship with Jesus Christ. You must ask Him to forgive you from your sins, to come into your heart, and to find a home within you (See 1John 1:8-7). But this isn't the end. Next, you must seek to change from your past. The sins that Jesus has forgiven you for can no longer be a part of who you are. A true relationship with Jesus results in real change in your life (See 2 Corinthians 5:17). How will you know if you have truly changed? Others will see this change in you. You will not be saying the same words you used to say. You will not be visiting the same places you visited before. You will be a new person in Christ.

Before beginning this Bible study, take a few moments to talk to God. Ask Him to forgive you for the sins in your life. Ask Him to reveal His truth to you. As you wait on Him, the Holy Spirit will reveal areas in your life in which you need to make changes. Recognize these areas and strive to find out how to make these changes in your life. Remember, no one will be a perfect Christian. Jesus was the only perfect Christian on earth. God doesn't call us to be perfect. He calls us to strive for perfection. As long as we are striving to please Him in all that we do, He will continue to reside within our souls and lead us through life.

Now get ready to grow with me! God is ready and waiting! Let's not delay!

Make a Commitment

Let's start this study with a commitment statement. A promise to ourselves, our fellow bible study participants, and to God. Read and put your name in the commitment line below.

I, ____, am ready to dive into God's Word to discover, practice, and use the skills He has prepared for me. I pledge to spend time searching in God's Word, talking to God, listening to His leading, and sharing my knowledge with others in my class. I won't quit when it gets tough.

When discouraged, I will refocus and continue to stay at it. I want to grow in my relationship with God so I can be the mother God has called me to be.

One of the most important attributes of this Bible study is trust. Trust between you and every other participant in the study. Many of the conversations that will take place during the next few months will involve difficult topics. It is most imperative that you remain a faithful, trusting friend throughout every conversation that occurs within all aspects of this class. I encourage you to create a text message group for support and sharing throughout the week. Support doesn't have to be limited to the times you gather together weekly. Support and prompting throughout the week can also help you each grow as mothers and children of God. Being able to trust the members of your class will not only help you share truth but will allow other women in your class to feel comfortable to share their own truths. Before the end of this study, you will have developed deep relationships with these new sisters in Christ, one that will last a lifetime.

If you vow to keep all discussions with these beautiful women confidential and are willing to be vulnerable with them, please sign the confidentiality line below. Breaking this vow will not only cause pain to the women who trust you, it will also cause pain to God. He takes your commitments and vows extremely seriously.

______________________________ ____________________

Confidentiality signature Today's date

Mapping God's Word

Spending time with God daily is a top priority in this Bible study. Prayer is a major communication tool we can use to build our relationship with God. God has given us His Word to guide us through making major and minor decisions in life. The Bible is filled with promises, warnings, and stories that we can use to become more like Him.

Prayer is a very important part of communication with God. It is our way to let God know about us on so many levels. Our prayer life should incorporate time **rejoicing and praising Him** for all that He has so graciously given us, from our homes to the food on our table to our families to our jobs and so much more. Just thinking about all He has blessed me with builds within me an overwhelming desire to humbly fall on my knees and praise Him with all that I have. There are so many things in my life that I can be thankful for.

Another part of our prayer life should be **seeking His will for our lives**. Every day we make life decisions that reflect who we are, who we want to be, and what truly matters in our lives. Ask God to reveal to you His truths. Ask God to show you all that He has for you. Seek Him with all that you have within you.

The last but most important part of prayer is **listening**. God will speak to us in so many different ways. In my life, God has spoken to me through the voices of other people, billboard signs, the actions of those around me, and more. We must be diligent as we wait for Him to speak. Do I believe that God can speak to us audibly? Yes, I do. But there are so many other ways He will speak to us as well. Don't lose heart if you don't hear from Him. He is there. Just be patient, wait, and watch.

God's Word is our number one, most important communication tool. This is where we learn about Him. The only way we can become better wives, mothers, daughters, and friends is to know God more. God is all knowing. He is the author of life. He has equipped each of us with the ability to know Him on a personal level. He will not force you to grow deeper with Him. You must take the initiative to get to know Him on your own. Pick up the Bible and read it. Don't read it to just say you've read His Word. Read it to learn, grow, and understand Him.

I would like to introduce to you a process I use while reading the Bible. I call it mapping God's Word. This process helps me to grow deeper instead of just reading the scriptures. **Every word God has placed in the Bible is there for a reason**. If we just read the words but don't dig deeper, we may miss out on so much truth that He placed there for us. I will teach you how I use this mapping process. You can mirror my mapping, choose to use only parts of it, or use your own method. As long as you are reading scripture to grow deeper, any method will work.

Step 1: Choose which Translation You Prefer

One of the first things you need to do is to choose which translation of the Bible works best for you. There are many different translations out there. I'm old school when it comes to God's Word—I want a Bible I can hold in my hand. However, I know many women who use their phone or iPad with a downloaded app to read. Use whatever works best for you. I use the New International Version (NIV). When I graduated from high school, my church gave me a Bible as a gift. This Bible used the NIV translation. So I've just continued to use this translation to this day. In the last few years, I was introduced to an amazing website called Blue Letter Bible[4]. This also comes as an app. The app comes with several free translations included, but you can download other versions of the Bible too. This app is amazing. You have access to Bible dictionaries, thesauruses, concordances, commentaries, videos, and so much more.

**If you know of a good Bible app, be sure to share it with your Bible study group.*

Step 2: Copy the Scripture into Your Book

Next, rewrite the scripture word-for-word. See my example below for week 1. (This is also found in the appendix.)

"But He said to me. 'My grace is sufficient for you, for my power is made perfect in weakness.' Therefore I will boast all the more gladly about my weaknesses, so that Christ's power may rest on me. That is why, for Christ's sake, I delight in weakness, in insults, in hardships, in persecutions, in difficulties. For when I am weak, then I am strong. " 2 Corinthians 12: 9 – 10 (NIV)

Step 3: Map out the Verse

Next, I go back to the verse and map it out. These are the guidelines I have found that help me to visually see the verse. I'm a visual learner. Highlighters are my best friends. Don't feel obligated to map as I do. Use what works best for you.

Highlight what stands out

Box a promise to proclaim

Circle words to define
Underline any commands
X OUT any sins to stay away from

"But He said to me. 'My grace is sufficient for you, for my power is made perfect in weakness.' Therefore I will boast all the more gladly about my weaknesses, so that Christ's power may rest on me. That is why, for Christ's sake, I delight in weakness, in insults, in hardships, in persecutions, in difficulties. For when I am weak, then I am strong."

Step 4: Define Words

Use a Bible dictionary or concordance to look up definitions of any words you may have circled. The website or map I mentioned earlier has a dictionary and concordance. What I love about a concordance is the ability to look up the Greek (original version of the Bible). We can learn a lot about God's Word by going back to the original version. You may be surprised by the many different definitions of words that we use in the English language. This helps us gain a deeper understanding of God's Word. There are various Bible dictionaries, concordances, and thesauruses. Seek out what works best for you.

Step 5: Add Commentary Notes

Commentaries are created by men or women who have studied the Bible and then lay out what these scriptures mean to them. Now, remember this is person's opinion of God's Word. So be sure to look up the Greek to compare to what others have to say. You can also use the internet to research the meaning of the verse. Just be cautious of where you are gathering these commentaries from. Be sure they are trustworthy, parallel with the Greek version of God's Word, and parallel with your pastor(s) teachings. See my commentary for 2 Corinthians 12: 9 - 10 below:

Greek words for:
Grace = that which affords joy, pleasure, delight, sweetness, charm, loveliness; grace of speech
Sufficient = to be possessed of unfailing strength; to be strong, to suffice, to be enough; to be satisfied; to be content
Weaknesses = want of strength of the body or of the soul

Rest on me = to dwell = to take possession of...house, citizens, power of Christ upon one

(By David Guzik) God was responding to Paul's request. Instead of removing the thorn from Paul's life, God gave and would keep giving His grace to Paul. The grace given was sufficient to meet his needs. God was strengthening Paul under the load he was bearing, and God's strength would be evident in Paul's ability to overcome his own weakness. How was God's grace enough? God's grace met Paul's need because it expresses God's acceptance and pleasure in us. Plus, God's grace was available all the time. Lastly, God's grace could meet Paul's need because it was the very strength of God. Paul was taught all these things through this time of suffering. Paul's response proves his love and trust in God. His endurance is evidence that God's strength can and will help us to endure.

Step 6: Summary

After searching deeper, summarize what this verse means to you. Here is my summary of 2 Corinthians 12: 9 - 10 :

Thank you God for your grace. You pour down grace upon me, even when I don't deserve it. Just like Paul, Your grace can help me endure the struggles of life. My struggles are nothing compared to Paul's struggles. I want to be more like Paul. I want to have the strength and faith he possessed through you, God.

Step 7: Apply It to Your Life

Write out how this verse can be applied to your life. Each time I read over a verse, I can apply it to my life in different ways. Remember that each part of God's Word is applicable to our lives. It's okay if this verse is challenging for you. It's okay if you're not sure how to apply this verse in your life. Just write from your heart in full honesty. Here's how I applied 2 Corinthians 12:9 - 10:

> Lord, help me to remember your grace IS sufficient for me. No matter what I face, you are right there beside me through it all. You shower me with grace beyond grace so that I may endure.

Step 8: Pray It Back to God

From the knowledge you have gained, you now have a plan of action to apply this verse to your life; talk to God about it. Be thankful. He will lead you to these truths. Be willing to make a change in your life to live by His Word. Be open to whatever He has for you beyond what you have gained from this study. Be open and honest with Him. Here is my prayer to God after my study with 2 Corinthians 12: 9- 10:

Lord, I want to use my struggles in life to show evidence of your strength and power. Allow me to keep my eyes on You in all that I do. No matter what trial or struggle I am facing, I want YOU to be the center of it all. I will hide Your Word in my heart; so that I can remind myself to look to you. Thank You Father!

Now as I said before, use any part of this mapping process as you wish. Modify it to meet your needs. Skip what you do not find valuable for your studies. Add things that help you along. This process is just a guide. Do what you need to do to make it work for you.

You will find my entire mapping of 1 John 4:7-8 in Appendix A. Refer to this example as you learn to map God's Word in your own way!

I have included space in the book for you to map scripture. However, it may not be enough space for you to journal. Do not limit your studies and findings to the empty spaces in this book. Discover what works for you and go with it. Remember the deeper you dig into His Word, the closer to God you become.

Chapter 1

Contentment

But seek first his kingdom and his righteousness, and all these things will be given to you as well. (Matthew 6:33 NIV)

Day 1: Being Content

What does it mean to be content? According to *Merriam-Webster's Dictionary*, there are several meanings to the word.

- To satisfy the mind; to make quiet, so-as-to stop complaint or opposition; to appease; to make easy in any situation
- Rest or quietness of the mind in the present condition; satisfaction which holds the mind in peace

Okay, moms, let's be real. How many times a day are we *not* content? No peace for the weary. You go into the bathroom for a little peace and quiet, but somehow they find you! Anyone here know what I'm talking about? Those little fingers wiggling under the door. Or better yet, they just walk right on in. How about this one: You just told them to stop, and they deliberately disobey you. Can I get an amen? Don't tell me my kids were the only ones! Oh, and we can't forget everyone's favorite phrase: "I'm hungry. Can I have a snack?" They just ate lunch five minutes ago! And last but not least, the famous last words of every mother: "Leave your brother or sister alone!"

Then there are all the "Why?" questions. Every mother has heard the question "Why?" at least a trillion times. There are times we simply say, "Because I said so." Or better yet, we act like we didn't hear them—and then they get louder and move closer to us. We have no choice but to respond before the neighbors call and ask if everything is okay.

We all reach our highest level of frustration when our kids continue to push every button we own. At times, it is difficult to remain content when we just want our children to be still and obey. It's in these moments I am reminded of Proverbs 22:6. In all of Solomon's wisdom, he makes it simple and says, "Train up your children." Oh, such simple words with such a huge meaning. Our children need to see us angry, sad, happy, joyful—every emotion. How we respond in those moments is what trains our children. We train them to respond as we responded. If we yell, scream, or punch something when we are angry or upset, don't be surprised when your children do the exact same thing. You train them every second of every day with your voice, body language, and attitude.

So, super moms, how we react in every situation is vital to how we expect our children to respond in similar situations. How can we handle these moments of discontent without becoming a grump? Is it even possible? I'm here to tell you the absolute truth: not always. You are human, and you are going to sometimes feel discontent. Our ultimate question is, How do we handle the moments that cause us to be discontent? These are what I call teachable moments, moments that our children watch our every move. What will we say? How will we say it? What will we do? How will we do it? What we do and say, they will do and say. Did you read what I wrote? Your kids are going to repeat your words and actions to others outside of the home. Ouch—this could come back to bite you later!

Okay, let's take a moment to journal. Write below areas you struggle with as a mom. What circumstances leave you reacting in ways that you are not proud of? Remember, we are all in the same boat here. We all fail at times! So be honest. (Hint: You don't have to share this with anyone but yourself and God.)

Okay, so now you know what circumstances cause you to blow. It's important to recognize what pushes you over the edge. Knowing your boundaries helps you to be aware, make changes, and possibly soften the blow.

My major struggle is when I have asked my children to stop a behavior, and they continue to disobey me. It's in these moments that I have taught myself to follow the following steps.

1. **Stop, breathe, and pray.** As a young mom, I would stop and breathe, but I forgot the most important part. I needed to seek wisdom from God. Whatever I had tried so far was not working; I was not communicating to my children in a way that they would take me seriously. I needed heavenly guidance. I usually also pray for the Holy Spirit to rain upon me love, patience, and self-control! I need to keep my cool and speak with love to my child.

2. **Sit, make eye contact, and speak wisdom.** I take the time to sit with my children, make sure they hear me (no distractions—make eye contact), and talk it out. My kids are thirteen, seventeen, and nineteen years old. They can sit and have a conversation with me. I speak from my heart. I love these moments with my children. When my children were younger, I still followed these same steps. However, our conversations were not as deep. Once your child becomes of age the he or she understands right from wrong, take the time to talk it out with them.
3. **Ask forgiveness** If I screwed up, I ask my children to forgive me for my faults. Your children need to know that you are not perfect. When you mess up, take ownership. Lead by example! Show them how to be humble.

Journal below if you use a discipline method that works well for you. We can learn so much from each other. Also know that there is no perfect mom out there. Even if you have a method that works well for you, it's not foolproof. Be open to new ideas.

Day 2: Mapping God's Word

(See my example—Appendix A)

2 Corinthians 12:9-10

Write It Down and Map It Out

Define Words, Thesaurus, and Commentaries

Summary

Apply It to Your Life

Pray It Back to God

Day 3: Mapping God's Word

Philippians 4:11-13

Write It Down and Map It Out

Define Words, Thesaurus, and Commentaries

Summary

Apply It to Your Life

Pray It Back to God

Day 4: Mapping God's Word

1 Corinthians 10:13

Write It Down and Map It Out

Define Words, Thesaurus, and Commentaries

Summary

Apply It to Your Life

Pray It Back to God

CHAPTER 1 MEMORY VERSE

Pick one of the verses you mapped this week to memorize. Rewrite the verse you have chosen below. Located in appendix B you will find suggestions on how to memorize scripture. Repetition...repetition is the key! The more you SEE the verse, HEAR the verse, and SAY the verse, the quicker you will memorize it! Each week you will be adding another memory verse to the list.

Chapter 1 memory verse:

CHAPTER 1 REVIEW

Day 1: Being Content

If you would like to share with your group, write a statement below that describes your struggles with being content as a woman.

If you would like to share with your group, write a statement below that describes your struggles with being a mom.

Would you like to share with your group this week about a strategy you use to remain calm in struggling circumstances? If so, write below what you would like to share.

Day 2 thru 4: Mapping God's Word

Pick one of the verses from this week to share with your class. Pick the verse that spoke the most to you. Look back over your map for this verse. Be prepared to share how you have applied or plan on applying this verse to your life.

Chapter 2

Jochebed

Now a man of the tribe of Levi married a Levite woman, and she became pregnant and gave birth to a son. When she saw that he was a fine child, she hid him for three months. (Exodus 2:1–2 NIV)

Jochebed

The Virtue of Total Trust in God

Look up the scriptures below about Jochebed, the mother of Aaron, Miriam, and Moses. She lived in a time of great sorrow for the Israelites. Pharaoh ordered that all newborn males be killed. She had to hide Moses with the hope that God would spare his life. We don't read much about her husband in the scriptures, but we do learn much about the life of Moses, Aaron, and Miriam. Looking at their lives, we can see how Jochebed and her husband raised their children. These scriptures hold many faith builders to pass down to your children and grandchildren.

Day 1

- **Exodus 1: 8-22 Jochebed's era**
    - o Why did the new king over Egypt choose to deal harshly with them?

- Was the king successful in his efforts to kill Moses? ____________________
- What did the king ask of the Hebrew mid-wives?

- Verse 17: Why did the mid-wives not follow the kings' instructions?

    - God blessed the mid-wives for their obedience. How were they blessed?

- What does the name Jochebed mean?

Day 2

- **Exodus 2: 1- 10 Moses and Miriam**
    - Describe the birth and first few months of Moses' life. Be specific on how God worked in his life.

- **Exodus 2: 11 – (chapter) 14 Jochebed's heritage at work!**
  - Spend time today reading through the stories of Moses, Aaron, and Miriam. Jot down anything you find of value to our study.

Day 3

- **Exodus 20: 20 – 21 Miriam sings and leads**
  - WhatdidMariamdotogiveGodpraise?______________________________
  - Rewrite her song lyrics below:
  - What do you think her song lyrics are referring too?
- **Numbers 12: 1 – 16 Children not seeing eye to eye**
  - What caused all of Jochebed's children to start arguing?
  - How did God handle the argument? Why do you think He spoke such words?

- Verse 10: What happened to Miriam when the glory of God departed?

- Aaron spoke up for his sister to Moses. Then Moses spoke up for his sister to God. How did God respond?

Day 4

- **Let's evaluate each of Jochebed's children**
  - Moses:
    - Moses became one of the greatest national leader's the world has ever known. He never felt as if he had the best ability to speak. He had quite a start at life; grew up with a mother who really wasn't his; was called to stand up for his true heritage; had the privilege of being in the presence of God; stood up with the assistance of his brother to the most powerful man of Egypt…keep adding to his life: (check out Hebrews 11:23)
    - Add your notes below:

- Aaron:
    - The oldest brother in the family. He had to take a backseat to Moses; heard the voice of God; obeyed God even when he may not have wanted to hear God's bidding…add to Aaron's list:
    - Add your notes below:

- Miriam:
    - The one sister in the family. She stood by her mother's side; assisting her mother in the safety of her youngest brother. She played such a key part in Moses' safe birth, but she had to take a backseat to Moses… continue to add to her story:
    - Add your notes below:

Here is a little bit about Jochebed from the author...

Jochebed was a Levite woman living under the authority of Pharaoh, an Egyptian ruler. Her life was no piece of cake. She was married to Amram, her nephew. We don't hear much about her husband. However, we learn a lot about Jochebed. She had three children: Aaron, Miriam, and Moses. The love she had for her children is evident in her steadfast actions to save Moses's life.

Pharaoh had such a fear of the Israelite people that he implemented a rule to control their population: the murder of innocent baby boys. While keeping Moses hidden, Jochebed placed her entire household in danger.

> And when she saw him that he was a goodly child,
> she hid him 3 months. (Exodus 2:2 KJV)

I'm not sure what the definition of *goodly* is. I consider it to be describing Moses as a pleasant, easygoing baby. Every mother dreams of a child like this. I can't even imagine Jochebed's fear that one of the soldiers would discover her secret, but she kept him despite those fears.

When she could hide him no longer, she knew she must let him go. Oh, the pain she must have endured, giving up her child with the hope that God would take care of him. And then to have Pharaoh's wife allow her, even pay her, to feed him. What a pleasant yet awful experience. Jochebed knew that one day she would have to trust God 100 percent with Moses's care. She had to release him to the Pharaoh's palace unknowing what would happen to him. She had to let him go and trust God.

What can we learn from Jochebed's story?

1. Jochebed believed God was **faithful**.
2. Jochebed instilled **leadership** skills in her children.
3. Jochebed **released** her children back to God.

CHAPTER 1 & 2 MEMORY VERSES

Rewrite your memory verse from chapter one below. I have given you your memory verse for chapter 2. Chose which translation you would prefer to use for this verse. Copy it below! Happy memorizing!

Chapter 1 memory verse:
Chapter 2 memory verse: Hebrews 11:23

CHAPTER 2 REVIEW

Jochebed

1. Did our character this week have a relationship with God? If so, describe that relationship. Include any changes that may have occurred with this relationship.

2. Describe this woman's character. What can we learn from her about faith, love, marriage, being a mother, grief, strength, perseverance, and more.

3. List an example of how this woman handled a specific struggle. Pay attention to details. These details help teach us right steps verses wrong steps to take.

4. What can we learn about being a wife or mother from this woman's story?

Chapter 3

Hold true to God's Word

Do your best to present yourself to God as one approved; a worker who does not need to be ashamed and who correctly handles the word of truth. (2 Timothy 2:15 NIV)

Day 1 : Hold True to God's Word

When I rededicated my life to Christ before my senior year of high school, I knew there was more to being a Christian than simply accepting Christ as my Savior. I needed to make a life change. I must change the way I talk, the places I visited (or at least the reason I visited them), the people I chose to call my friends, the way I reacted to situations, and the way I carried myself. The Holy Spirit implored me to search the scriptures to find the truth to these changes I needed to make.

Have you ever read something in scripture that caused you to question its meaning? Boy, I have! Especially parts of the Old Testament. He begot him, who begot him, who begot him. I mean, why does that even matter?

It's actually extremely important. These verses set up the family line from Adam and Eve to Jesus. I was never much of a history buff until I started reading the Bible. The only way I knew the truth about scripture was to seek out guidance from others that knew more than me. I didn't actually start deeply studying the Word until I was in my thirties. And I learn more and more about living a Godly life as I continue to study it.

Too many people claim to be Christians, but they do not spend time in God's Word. You must study His Word to learn His Ways so you may become more like Him. Saying you're a Christian and living like a Christian are two different things. So, what can the scriptures do for you?

The scriptures can bring you joy. Christians experience a joy beyond what the world has to offer. This joy is unspeakable joy. Its true identity can only be found in God's Word. This joy is our strength to endure when the world says to quit.

> These things I have spoken to you, that my joy may be in you, and that your joy may be full. (John 15:11)

The scriptures will lead you to the truth. The world hides the truth from us. Satan doesn't want you to know that there is hope in the midst of despair. In fact, Satan will surround you with people who lead you down the path of hopelessness. If he can destroy your hope, then he has you right where he wants you. Ladies, God is our hope. In the scriptures, we find stories and parables that lead to endurance, peace, longsuffering, and so much more. All you have to do is open and read!

The Word is so essential to our survival that David compared it to a tree planted by the river (Psalm 1:2–3). And Jesus Himself tells us, "Man shall not live by bread alone, but by every word that comes from the mouth of God" (Matthew 4:4). Simon Peter replies to Jesus, "Lord to whom shall we go? You have the words to eternal life" (John 6:68). God's Word is vital to our survival, so what shall we do?

Well, right now you are taking this Bible study class—hence the word *Bible*. You are in His Word daily. You not only are reading His Word, but you are studying it. Every week, you search scriptures to find out truth about Him. You discuss these verses with other women. You may not always agree upon the meanings, but you are learning and growing. It is essential that your children see you striving to learn more and draw closer to Jesus. They need to know that you seek God, who has your number one priority. You may even stop an activity to make sure you get your time in with God daily. I can't emphasize this enough: don't put it off; be diligent about spending time in His Word.

For many years, I was the director of a children's ministry at my church. I wrote the lessons, created the scheduling, set up teachers, and advertised events. My best friend, Annette, worked alongside me during this amazing growth period of my life. Before becoming the director of the program, my Bible time was hit or miss. Unfortunately, most of the time it was a miss. I had tons of excuses, but none of them were good! I knew that I needed to be grounded in His Word so I could be used for His glory!

I made a lot of mistakes in those early years of ministry. Many times I was faced with trials, and I penciled it out instead of standing on His Word as my anchor. Each time I tried to face the trials on my own, I was soon put flat on my face. I then picked myself up, asked for forgiveness, and moved on. Each mistake I made caused me to grow closer to God. But I hurt people during this time. I had confrontation with teachers that I was not biblically prepared to handle. Most teachers understood, and together we grew in the knowledge of God. Some didn't, however. They grew bitter toward me, and I had to withstand this consequence—all because I was not seeking God's ways in all that I did.

Hindsight is twenty-twenty, so learn from my mistakes. Seek first the kingdom of God, and everything else will fall together around you. It's such a simple thing to do, but we make it so complicated. All God asks is that we seek Him! One way to seek Him is by reading His Word. God is faithful to those who follow Him.

Think about this for a moment. How many of you are living your life based on the lessons you learned as a child? From Sunday school, family members, or past youth leaders, the lessons they taught us were essential in setting up our foundation. But now you are on the rock, you need to go deeper. There is no more relying on the lessons we learned from the past to lead us where we are now. If you want to grow in God, then you must grow deeper!

On the flip side, some of you didn't grow up with memories of Sunday School lessons, or family members who mentored you in Christ along the way. Use the lack from your past as motivation to break the cycle and make your relationship with Christ visual to those around you.

Just like I previously stated, I did not start searching scriptures for the history of the Old Testament till I was in my thirties. I wanted to grow deeper, and this was one of the ways I could learn more about God. I spent many years researching the history and genealogy of Jesus. I read and reread the stories of the Israelites being set free from Egyptian slavery and being led to the promised land. There is so much we can learn from their mistakes and triumphs. I studied the book of Proverbs to truly see what the wisest man on earth had to tell me. There are some major truths located in Proverbs that would blow the socks off your feet. But if you sit around and wait for the preacher to preach about it, or for someone to lead a Sunday school class about it, you are missing out on so much! God wants to see us work at it on our own.

You will struggle. I'm just being honest. You will read some scriptures, and then reread them over and over until you can grasp the understanding. And then you may still struggle with understanding them. Seek out guidance! Stop using the excuse that you don't have time, or that you haven't been a Christian long enough to go deeper. Those are all lies from Satan.

Every Sunday morning our pastor, James Fry, leads the congregation through a saying. It goes like this.

> This is my Bible; it's God's infallible Word. I am who it says I am, I have what it says I have, and I can do what it says I can do. Today I will be taught the Word of God. I'm about to receive the incorruptible, indestructible, ever-living seed of the Word of God. My mind is alert, my heart is receptive, and I will never be the same in Jesus's name.

What if I recited this every time I opened God's Word? What if I approached His Word with confidence and a drive to seek His Ways, to know him in a much more intimate way? Trust me: you will be changed, but you will also be filled with joy. Don't delay—start taking God's Word serious right this very moment! Don't just read it to check off a list of things to do. Actually study it to grow closer to Him than you have ever been in your life. It's worth the time, and it's worth the struggle. Just do it!

Day 2: Mapping God's Word

2 Timothy 3:16 - 17

Write It Down and Map It Out

Define Words, Thesaurus, and Commentaries

Summary

Apply It to Your Life

Pray It Back to God

Day 3: Mapping God's Word

John 8:31 - 32

Write It Down and Map It Out

Define Words, Thesaurus, and Commentaries

Summary

Apply It to Your Life

Pray It Back to God

Day 4: Mapping God's Word

Romans 10:17

Write It Down and Map It Out

Define Words, Thesaurus, and Commentaries

Summary

Apply It to Your Life

Pray It Back to God

CHAPTER 1 THRU 3 MEMORY VERSES

Rewrite your memory verses from chapter one and two below. Pick one of the verses you mapped this week to memorize. Rewrite the verse you have chosen below in chapter 3's memory verse section.

Chapter 1 memory verse:
Chapter 2 memory verse: Hebrews 11:23
Chapter 3 memory verse:

CHAPTER 3 REVIEW

Day 1: Hold True to God's Word

What parts of scripture do you read that cause you to ask questions? Did you seek out an answer to these questions? If so, can you share what you learned with the class? We can learn from each other!

How much time do you spend in God's Word weekly? Do you have a schedule that you try to follow? A certain time? A certain amount of time? Or do you need to create a weekly schedule to be in God's Word? What is stopping you from making His Word a priority in your life? Share with each other this week during class on what works for you. What keeps you in His Word?

Do you have a story to share this week when God put you in a situation where you were successful or unsuccessful? I shared a few of my unsuccessful stories because I want you to know that you won't be perfect, and that's okay! Learn from your mistakes, make better choices, and grow!

Day 2 thru 4: Mapping God's Word

Pick one of the verses from this week to share with your class. Pick the verse that spoke the most to you. Look back over your map for this verse. Be prepared to share how you have applied or plan on applying this verse to your life.

Chapter 4

Ruth

"But Ruth replied, 'Don't urge me to leave you or to turn back
from you. Where you go I will go, and where you stay I will stay.
Your people shall be my people and your God my God."
Ruth 1:16 NIV

Ruth

Inspired by Others

Inspired by Others

Look up the scriptures below about Ruth. Ruth left everything she knew to take care of her mother-in-law. Be honest: When faced with Ruth's situation, what would you have done? We all have different situations with our families. Some of us are extremely close to our families, and we can't imagine life without them. Others are not close to their families at all. Do you think this played a role in Ruth's decision to follow Naomi back to a land she never knew? Serving a God she never knew before? Was there something different with Naomi's family? Something that inspired Ruth? Let's find out!

Day 1

Today we will begin in Ruth chapter 1. Who is Ruth anyway? And how does she find herself in this crazy and unfair situation?

- Ruth 1: 1 – 5
  - o Where were Elimelek, Naomi, and their 2 sons from? _______________

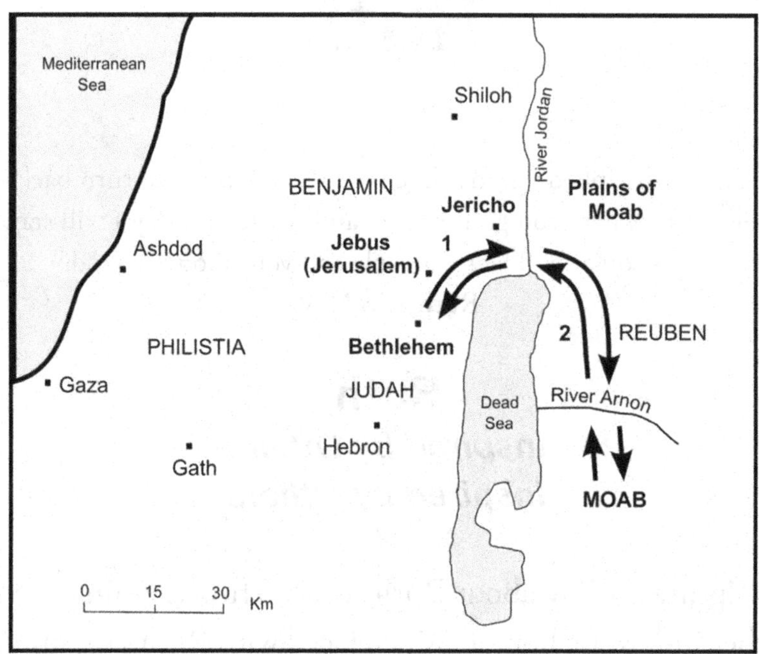

(*The Bible Journey by* Chris & Jenifer Taylor)

- This journey would have taken them quite some /time! Why did they leave their homeland?

- How long did they live in Moab before the 2 sons married? ______
  - How do you think Naomi felt about her sons marrying Moabite women?

- Ruth 1: 6-7
  - What caused Naomi to want to return to her homeland?
    - What do you think, beyond what scriptures share with us, was a drive for her to return to her homeland?
  - What was custom for widowed women in these times? (Your going to have to do some studying beyond God's Word) 😊

- Ruth 1: 8-14
  - Naomi pleads with her daughters-in-law to return home. What reason does she give them to return home?

- Did Orpah and Ruth quickly return to their homes? Describe in detail how they each respond.

- In verse 13, Naomi says, "it is more bitter for me than for you, because the Lord's hand has turned against me!" What is she talking about?

- Ruth 1: 15-18
  - Describe how Ruth responded to Naomi. Pay close attention to each detail of their conversation! How important was it to Ruth that she remain with Naomi?

  - What does this tell us about Ruth's personality? What type of a person was she?

- Ruth 1: 19 - 22
  - Naomi returned home a completely broken woman. Ruth stood by her side through it all. In your mind, describe a visual picture of the relationship between Naomi and Ruth. As they traveled, what were their days like?

Day 2

So Naomi and Ruth have returned to Bethlehem, just as the barley harvest was to begin. (FYI: God's timing is always just right!)

- Ruth 2: 1 – 13
  - Naomi and Ruth need to find food. It was uncommon for women to work outside of the home, and they had no man to find work. So where does Ruth go to get food? ______________________________
    - Who owned this field? ________________
    - Why is this significant to the story?
  - Did Ruth ask permission to glean from this field? Which verse do you find the answer? ____
  - In verse 4, Boaz returns from Bethlehem and greets his workers. What can we learn about Boaz from how he greets his workers?
  - Boaz has compassion upon Ruth…why?
- Ruth 2: 14 - 23
  - What kind act did Boaz give to Ruth at mealtime? How do you think his workers felt about this kindness?

- Boaz looked out for Ruth. He even told his workers to look over her, and grant her more grain. His kindness towards her is very comparable to how Jesus showed kindness to so many while He was here on earth. List examples of Jesus' kindness being comparable to the kindness Boaz portrayed.

- Through Boaz, God provided more than enough food for Naomi and Ruth. Do you have examples in your life when God used a Boaz to provide more than enough for you and your family? If so, tell us about it!

- What was Naomi's response when Ruth told her about Boaz' kindness?

    - In verse 20, Naomi refers to Boaz as a "guardian redeemer" of the family. What does this mean?

Day 3

God has provided for Ruth and Naomi through the kindness and compassion of Boaz. Let's continue to read and see how this kindness turns into love.

- Ruth 3: 1-5
  - Naomi sets up Ruth for Boaz. What specifically does she tell Ruth to do?
    - Was this custom in these times? Dig and see what you can find out!

- Ruth 3: 6-11
  - Did Naomi's plan work? ________
  - In verse 10, Boaz finds favor with Ruth because she did not go out to find a young man to marry, but she came to him—an older man. He uses the same phrase here as he used when he greeted his servants in chapter 2. What was this phrase? ________________________________
  - He promises Ruth to make sure everyone knows of her kindness. I would say we already have quite a love story here ☺

- Ruth 3: 12-18
  - Just when we thought our love story couldn't get better…we could hear wedding bells…Boaz puts a blow into the whole story. What does he tell Ruth?
  - Ruth left in the morning before anyone could see her. But she didn't leave empty handed. What did Boaz give her to take home to her mother-in-law?

- What was Naomi's response to Boaz' gift?

Day 4

Look back over all that we have read in Ruth so far. Look where she came from to where she is now. She remained faithful to the health and well-being of her mother-in-law, and God has blessed her. The ending is the best. Let's finish it up today!

- Ruth 4: 1-12
    - Boaz meets up with this other relative. He also calls who else to witness this meeting?
    - Boaz had a plan. His plan did not start with his deepest desire…to marry Ruth. How did his plan lay out?
        - FYI: When the Isrealites entered the promise land, Joshua divided the land among the tribes and family groups. God intended that the land stay within these original groups. Read Leviticus 25: 8 – 17 to see how God set up the land to remain in these same groups.
        - 50 years is a long time. So, God had also set up a plan, the one Boaz used, to use the kinsman-redeemer to full-fill his plan.

- Ruth 4: 13-23
  - Boaz and Ruth marry! But the story doesn't stop here. They have a son. What is the son's name? ______________________________ Who named him? ____________________________
  - Reread Naomi's words in Ruth 1: 20-21. Compare these words to where she is now. An excellent example to never give up!

  - The lineage of their son is described at the very end of this chapter. Rewrite it below. WOW!

    - What if Ruth had not come back with Naomi? What if she would have staid in Moab to follow the traditions and marry a man from her home town? Her decision had a huge impact on our lives today. When we follow God's leading, it's all a part of a bigger plan. ☺

Here is a little bit about Ruth...

Inspired by Others

Ruth inhabited a foreign homeland, endured the pain and agony of working to supply food for herself and Naomi, and never complained or gave in. Are you ready to sign up for any of these? Most of us wouldn't want to do one of these things, let alone all of them. Ruth's life is a total amazement to me. She loved without expecting anything in return. She is the perfect example of the love of Christ.

When Ruth became a young widow, I wonder what went through her mind. There is not much information given to us about her grieving period. I'm sure she went through some very troubling times. She never seemed to complain about her situation. She simply continued to endure. It was as if she knew there was hope that she would be okay. When she had married into the family, the family was wealthy and well aboded. But now that she was widowed, they had no choice but to drop to the bottom of the social ring.

Being from Moab, she had not been brought up learning about the love of God. Her new in-law family shared His love with her, and she seemed to embrace it. I'm sure she watched as Naomi cared for her family with love, striving to be a good wife and mother. When tragedy struck the family, it was Ruth who kept everything together. Even in her short time of salvation, God used her to save others. God knew she was the right woman for this family. Just like in our situations, He always knows what lies before us!

Once she entered Bethlehem, she worked at the bottom of the social ring. She didn't seem to be bothered by this in anyway. She simply continued every day to do what she had to do to survive. Her boss, Boaz, was a gentle and loving man. He even had his workers leave extra wheat for her to collect to keep for her table. He protected her and supplied for her. He could see her beauty inside and out. God had even worked out the lineage to so that they could be wed. Ruth went from rags to riches!

Here is what can we learn from Ruth.

1. Ruth's **love** for her mother-in-law goes beyond anything anyone ever asked of her.

   > But Ruth said, "Do not urge me to leave you or to return from following you. For where you go I will go, and where you lodge I will lodge. Your people will be my people, and your God my God." (Ruth 1:16)

2. Ruth did what she had to survive, **without complaint or protest**, not only for herself but for Naomi as well.

   > And Ruth the Moabite said to Naomi, "Let me go to the fields and glean among the ears of grain after him whose sight I shall find favor." (Ruth 2:2)

CHAPTER 1 THRU 4 MEMORY VERSES

Rewrite your memory verses from previous chapters below. I have given you your memory verse for chapter 4. Chose which translation you would prefer to use for this verse. Copy it below! Happy memorizing!

Chapter 1 memory verse:
Chapter 2 memory verse: Hebrews 11:23
Chapter 3 memory verse:
Chapter 4 memory verse: Ruth 1:16

CHAPTER 4 REVIEW

Ruth

1. Did our character this week have a relationship with God? If so, describe that relationship. Include any changes that may have occurred with this relationship.

2. Describe this woman's character. What can we learn from her about faith, love, marriage, being a mother, grief, strength, perseverance, and more.

3. List an example of how this woman handled a specific struggle. Pay attention to details. These details help teach us right steps verses wrong steps to take.

4. What can we learn about being a wife or mother from this woman's story?

Chapter 5

Releasing Our Children Back to God

Children are a heritage from the LORD, offspring a reward from him. Like arrows in the hands of a warrior are children born of one's youth. (Psalm 127:3–4 NIV)

Day 1: Releasing our children back to God

Moms, every child God has blessed you with is a gift, a uniquely designed mixture of you and your husband (or the child's biological parents). God creates children with their own plans in place. It is our job to teach them about God and the difference between right and wrong. God compares our children to arrows. God knows exactly where each arrow should be pointed. He knows the best timing for when the arrow should be moved and where it should be pointed.

Let's take a moment and think about these arrows God has blessed us with. I have 2 arrows that I was never able to touch. The 2 miscarriages I experienced in my life were not mistakes. Every child God grants us are blessings. I has taken me a long time to consider my miscarriages as a blessing. God's Word has been my guidance and strength in this area.

I also have 3 wonderful arrows right here on Earth. I recall times when my husband and I tried to control the bow. We would point the bow and arrow towards ideas of the world. For example, the emotional status of our child's heart, the spiritual choices they make, forms of discipline encouraged by the world, and many more. My point in all of this is that – WE hold the bow (our husbands first and us as a helper to our husbands). For me, that is a lot of pressure. What if I point the arrow the wrong direction? What if I pull back too far on the bowstring? When it's time to let our arrows go into the world will I have the arrow pointed in the right direction, the direction God had planned for my child? All these thoughts can create huge amounts of stress. Whose with me here?

As mothers, we not only want to teach and lead our children as infants, but we want to continue to hold their hands through every event they experience in life. My daughter turned eighteen in 2019, and I still want to be there in case she needs me. It's a mom thing. We want our children to succeed and follow God's ways in all things. She is now nineteen years old, when do I let her arrow fly away from me? Oh, if only we could help control her live forever.

And here it is…our number one fear. That our children will become corrupted by Satan's lies and turn from God. We diligently pray that our children will not be intrigued by Satan's playground. We spend so much time praying, teaching, and molding our children. We pray that Satan leaves our children alone—mind, body, and soul. Our prayers are from the deepest parts of our soul. We continually make things right with God and others. We want God to hear our prayers (James 5:16). During the young and teenage years, we do all we can to instill God's way in their lives. We take them to church, teach them how to pray, study scripture with them, and try to lead a righteous life. But there will come a day when your children need to be given opportunities to make their own choices—the day we send them out on their own. Yicks!

Every mother who has sent her little five-year-old to school on the first day of kindergarten (or earlier for preschool) knows exactly what I'm talking about. They go from being in our care twenty-four seven to being in the care of the school. Scary! We cry, use up tons of tissues, and wonder all day long how they are doing. When they come home, we bombard them with a million questions about their day. A little bit of us wants to hear them say, "I sure missed you, Mom." Then the day comes when they ask if they can have a sleepover at a friend's or relative's home. We don't let them go unless we feel 100 percent confident they will be loved and cared for while away from us. Then we say, "Sure," even though we mean, "Please stay home where I can protect you." Then we worry about them all night long. If you've been there, say 'Amen'!!

We had restrictions in place if our children wanted to spend time outside of our home. For our household, our children could only stay at a friend's house if all of the following standards were met.

1. We had to know the parents well, meaning we had conversations with the parents face-to-face!
2. Before the sleepover, we had to have a face-to-face or phone conversation about the event.
3. We had to set up a 'plan of escape' if our child needed us. If for some reason our child needed us to come get them, we created a plan. Usually this meant at around 9:00 P.M. we would give them a call. If they were having a great time and felt safe, we would chat for a few minutes then hang up. If they needed us to come get them, we would ask and they would just say 'yes'. We didn't ask details. They knew we were on our way to get them.

Needless to say, my kids only asked to stay the night if they knew all the above was in place. So, if they came to ask us to stay away from our protection, they already had a plan in place for Curt or I to speak with the other adults involved.

As our children grow older, they will want to adventure out more. They ask to play sports, where we must trust them with coaches and helpers. They may ask to go on vacation with family or friends. This really flips the concern switch because they will be farther away from us. What if they are hurt and need us? We think of the worst possible scenario in our minds, and then we convince ourselves that it's a bad idea. They can't survive without us; they need us to be close to them always. Our worries become overwhelmed with the what-ifs?

If your children are still very young, you may not have experienced any of the above yet. I'm sure you have thought about it. Possibly you are unsure what you would say or do. However, if you have been put in these situations, describe how you have handled these situations. Your advice may help other mommas who need help in this area.

Do you and your husband have boundaries set for your children when they ask to leave your presence, participating in something beyond your home? If so, write what procedures you use below.

Flip back and take a look at our study on Jochebed. Just like she had to trust God with her son Moses, we must trust God with our children too. We must release them into the safety of His protection. Easier said than done, I know. Think about how much faith Jochebed had to have to release Moses to the hands of Pharaoh's daughter. Think of how hard this must have been. She had no choice. If she wanted Moses to live, she had to let go and let God.

Returning your children to God is so much more than the little children baptism that occurs at many churches. At these ceremonies, our children are baptized and prayed over by the pastor and elders. They pray a prayer that commits our children to God. They ask that they, parents, and the congregation members work together to teach the children in the ways of the Lord. We then usually take pictures and eat cake! We celebrate this joyous occasion knowing God has our children in His hands.

But these ceremonies occur before our children are old enough to make the decision to accept Jesus Christ as their personal Savior. I am not saying you shouldn't have you children dedicated to God. What I am saying is this is not enough! From the day we dedicate our children to God, Satan sees this as an opportunity to intercede into our children's lives. Satan wants to make sure your child never accepts Jesus. He wants your children to live miserable, depressed, frustrated, and lost lives. We must spent many hours in prayer, teaching and equipping our children to know, understand, and apply God's Word to their lives. This must be our number one goal. Little by little, as our children grow, we must stop trying to control the bow and allow God to have complete control of it.

Now, don't get me wrong: children need to earn the trust of their parents in order to earn freedom. A plan needs to be put into place between the parents and children as to earning their "Can I ...?" moments. We can only let go and allow our children more freedom (away from our fold) once the child has demonstrated they understand and have earned the right to this freedom. God is very adamant about children obeying their parents (Ephesians 6:1). Hence discipline, which is another topic for itself. We just can't decide one day that our children are ready for the world, even small parts of it, if we are unsure of their understanding of the world.

Before our children can participate in activities beyond our household, they have responsibilities they must accomplish first. Do you and your husband have ways your children 'earn their freedom' to do things with family or friends away from you control? If so, list them below:

Letting go is the hardest part of motherhood. We must continue to pray for our children and be there to pick them up then they fall. But at some point, hopefully they will connect with God, and He will begin to lead them on the path He has laid out for them. We must trust God to equip them along the way with all that they need and trust He will lead us to them when the time is right. We must back off and allow God to lead through the Holy Spirit. You will always be their mom, and you will always be there for them. As long as they know they have their parents, and God, they will be okay.

Side note: I realize not everyone is living in the world I described above. There are mommas reading through this week's lesson with guilt, sorrow, and frustration. You may have felt you did everything you could, and your child has fallen prey to Satan. Or you may feel guilty. You feel you didn't do enough to keep your child from Satan's grasp. Mommas read this and believe it: As moms we can only do what we can do, then it is up to our children to make the right choices. Don't beat yourself up because your child went astray. Seek Gods Will for how He would have you handle this relationship between your child and yourself. God knows more about your child than you do. He knows every thought, every action, every need, every wish, and every desire they have. Trust Him to lead you! And let your group know you need prayer. Prayer is a mighty and powerful thing. Use your class as prayer warriors to help you hear and obey the Holy Spirit, and to help your child do the same.

Day 2: Mapping God's Word

Proverbs 3: 5 - 6

Write It Down and Map It Out

Define Words, Thesaurus, and Commentaries

Summary

Apply It to Your Life

Pray It Back to God

Day 3: Mapping God's Word

Philippians 1:6

Write It Down and Map It Out

Define Words, Thesaurus, and Commentaries

Summary

Apply It to Your Life

Pray It Back to God

Day 4: Mapping God's Word

Joshua 1:9

Write It Down and Map It Out

Define Words, Thesaurus, and Commentaries

Summary

Apply It to Your Life

Pray It Back to God

CHAPTER 1 THRU 5 MEMORY VERSES

Rewrite your memory verses from previous chapters below. Pick one of the verses you mapped this week to memorize. Rewrite the verse you have chosen below in chapter 5's section.

Chapter 1 memory verse:
Chapter 2 memory verse: Hebrews 11:23
Chapter 3 memory verse:
Chapter 4 memory verse: Ruth 1:16

Chapter 5 memory verse:

Day 1: Releasing Our Children Back to God

Look back over the points in this lesson where you added information about the methods you use in your household for sleepovers, your children spending time away from your presence, and requirements to make all these opportunities work. Be ready to share your experiences with your class.

What level of anxiety do you feel thinking about letting your children out of your protective circle?

Have you found a strategy that works well when dealing with this type of anxiety?

Please be respectful of everyone in your Bible study. Each and every one of us deals with life in many different aspects. There are a lot of very healthy ways to deal with anxiety, but there are also unhealthy ways too. Be quick to listen and slow to speak as you share at this week's class. Speak to uplift, not to discourage anyone. What may work for one family may not work sufficiently for another, and there is nothing wrong with that!

Day 2 thru 4: Mapping God's Word

Pick one of the verses from this week to share with your class. Pick the verse that spoke the most to you. Look back over your map for this verse. Be prepared to share how you have applied or plan on applying this verse to your life.

Chapter 6

Eve

But I am afraid that just as Eve was deceived by the serpent's cunning, your minds may somehow be led astray from your sincere and pure devotion to Christ. (2 Corinthians 11:3 NIV)

Eve

The first mother with a troubled child

Eve's life started out great. In fact, she was made in the image of God. She walked each day with God and her husband, Adam. They lived in the Garden of Eden, a place of beauty, freedom, and love. With all her love, compassion, and desire to please, she was the perfect person to be tempted by Satan. When tempted, she failed. Not only did she fail, but she dragged her husband into the mess too. She was the first person to sin, and her child was the first child to murder his own brother. Things started out great but quickly went downhill. How did she handle all the stress and craziness? How did God handle all this craziness? There's a lot we can learn from this woman, Eve.

Day 1

- Genesis 2: 18 – 25 God created Eve
    - Why did God create Eve? What was His motivation?

- Verse 23: What does Adam say about Eve?

    - What do you think he, Adam, means by these words? Look up and read a few text commentaries about this verse.

- Verse 24 – 25: These verses are used a lot when couples get married. What do these verses mean to you? How do they relate to you and your spouse?

    - Dig deeper into these scriptures to find the true meaning for you. Define words, use bible concordance, and read commentaries.

Day 2

- Genesis 3: 1- 7 Eve is deceived by the serpent
    - Verse 1: What words are used by the serpent to deceive Eve?

        - Why was this such a crafty way to word the question?

- Verse 2 – 3: How does Eve answer the serpent?

- Verse 4 – 5: The serpent as an answer for her response. He tempts her by questioning what God had commanded. Think about your own life. Is there a time in your life that 'the serpent' challenges your faith and belief in God? Think, and then write below an example from your own life.

- Verse 6 – 7: Eve, along with her husband, both fail…they disobey God and gave into the temptation set before them from the serpent. What happens as a result?

- Genesis 3: 8 – 15 Consequences of their choices
  - Verses 8 – 9: What do Adam and Eve do when God calls to them? Keep in mind, before this day Adam and Eve would spend much time walking and talking through the garden with God. But that all changes once they disobey God.

  - Verses 10 – 13: She…he…it…made me do it!
    - Why didn't Eve or Adam admit to their wrong? (Do some digging and research to see what you can find out about this.)

- Verses 14 – 15: Punishment
    - How is the serpent punished? Why do you think God punished him?

Day 3

- Genesis 3: 16 God punishes Eve for eating from the tree of knowledge
    - What was Eve's consequence from eating this fruit?
    - Does this leave you with any questions about God's punishments? If so, describe below.
- Genesis 3: 17 – 29 Adam is punished
    - What is Adam's punishment for disobeying?
- Genesis 3: 20 – 24 Good and evil
    - What does Eve mean? ______________________________
    - God makes clothing for Adam and Eve. Do you find it interesting that God, even after punishing them, still provides for them?

- God removes Adam and Eve from the Garden of Eden. What do verses 22 – 24 mean to you? (Do some digging to find out)

Day 4

- Genesis 4: 1 – 2 Cain and Abel
  - Which child was born first? ______________________________
    - Abel was a ________________________ of ______________________
    - Cain loved to work with the ______________________________.

- Genesis 4: 3 – 5 God had regard for one offspring but not the other
  - What offering did Cain bring before God?
  - What offering did Abel bring before God?
  - How did God react to both offerings?
    - Cain:

- Abel:

  - We are not told how Abel reacted, but what did Cain do?

There are so many who believe that God's reaction to Cain's offering was because he did not offer an animal. But God accepted seed offerings along with animal offerings in these times. The problem with Cain's offering is addressed in the following scriptures.

- Genesis 4: 6 – 7 Cain is angry with God
  - God approached Cain in love. He knew that Cain was upset. What did God ask Cain? ____
    - God warned Cain that sin was at his door. What do you think He met by this?

- Genesis 4: 8 – 16 Cain murders Abel
  - How does the murder of Abel play out?

  - o Describe the conversation between Cain and God after the murder takes place. What parallels can you find from Adam and Eve's sin in the Garden?

- Genesis 4: 17 -24 Cain's heritage
  - o Read through these verses. Is there anything disturbing about Cain's lineage?

- Genesis 4: 25 – 26 Seth is born
  - o Adam and Eve had more than 3 children. However, Seth's birth was the last worthy of mentioning in the Bible. Why?

  - o The birth of Seth brought a revival (of sorts) to the people. Why?

Here is a little bit about EVE...

First off, let's think a moment about the fact that Eve was created in God's own image. First He created Adam. But Adam could not get through this life on his own. He needed a helpmate, someone to see each situation from a different perspective. That's who we are, ladies. God made us in His own image, from the rib of man, yet with our own unique characteristics.

How many times have you noticed that men and women think so differently? Yeah, me too—a lot of times! God created us to be different. He gave jobs to men and He gave women jobs as well. One of those jobs is to bear children. Each of my children's pregnancies, along with deliveries, have their own unique stories to tell. Throughout each experience, God was by my side through it all.

Eve's firstborn, Cain, and Abel started out as blessings but quickly changed to destruction. Just like Satan was able to deceive Eve, he moved in on her children too. How devastating for Adam and Eve! I cannot imagine the pain they experienced knowing the loss of one son by death and the other by distance. The pain of losing a child is an unbearable experience. I lost two children to miscarriages; I was never able to get to know them before God took them to heaven. I'm sure the pain of losing a child you were able to nurture, love, and create a relationship with must be so much more painful than what I experienced.

Have you experienced a loss of a child? If you would like to share any of your journey with your class, take time to write out your story to share. Do not feel obligated to share. Not only is writing out this part of your journey healthy for you, but sharing it with others is healing! I haven't left space in the book for your story. Use a separate journal to write down your thoughts.

What can we learn from Eve's story?

1. Eve was made in **God's image** and made to be a **helpmate** for Adam.
2. We don't learn a lot about how Eve raised her children. We know she was not perfect, she was made with flesh just like we are. However, and she had to endure the pain of losing a child. God did bless her with more children. Despite Cain and Abel's decisions, Adam and Eve were entrusted with more children. Eve learned to endure despite pain and sorrow.

CHAPTER 1 THRU 6 MEMORY VERSES

Rewrite your memory verse from previous chapter below. I have given you your memory verse for chapter 6. Chose which translation you would prefer to use for this verse. Copy it below! Happy memorizing!

Chapter 1 memory verse:
Chapter 2 memory verse: Hebrews 11:23
Chapter 3 memory verse:
Chapter 4 memory verse: Ruth 1:16

Chapter 5 memory verse:
Chapter 6 memory verse: 2 Corinthians 11:3

CHAPTER 6 REVIEW

Eve

1. Did our character this week have a relationship with God? If so, describe that relationship. Include any changes that may have occurred with this relationship.

2. Describe this woman's character. What can we learn from her about faith, love, marriage, being a mother, grief, strength, perseverance, and more.

3. List an example of how this woman handled a specific struggle. Pay attention to details. These details help teach us right steps verses wrong steps to take.

4. What can we learn about being a wife or mother from this woman's story?

Chapter 7

Inspired by Others

Therefore encourage one another and build each other up, just as in fact you are doing. (1 Thessalonians 5:11 NIV)

Day 1: Inspired by Others

Over the past forty-three years of my life, I can remember so many different people who have inspired me to be the woman I am today. First off, my mom and dad deserve much credit. I never went without in my life. We were at church every

Sunday and most Wednesday evenings as well. As a kid, my mom was my Sunday school teacher as far back as I can remember. My dad was a lay pastor and would fill in for local pastors who were on vacation or needed a day off. He was never ordained as a pastor, but he would help out when needed. Both my mom and dad have been there for me countless times over the years.

My grandparents were perfect examples of love. They showed so much love toward their spouses—love beyond words or actions. In fact, my maternal grandpa, Don Peters, gave up everything to move into the nursing home with my grandma, Janet, when she had Alzheimer's. He tried to keep her at home for as long as possible, but the day came when that no longer worked. The only thing he kept was his truck, so he could drive places. What an example of true, selfless love. My grandfather amazed me with his dedication for my grandmother.

Many other men and women have inspired me to love unconditionally, forgive and let go of past hurts, learn from my mistakes but don't let them define me, and so much more. You can learn more about my inspiration from others by reading my acknowledgments page in the front of the book.

Make a list below of people who have inspired you to be better and more like Christ. Describe how their actions and words helped mold you into the woman you are today. The longer your list, the more blessed you are! The older you are, the longer your list will be as well. And as the years pass, a few of these people will slip your mind. Then something will happen, and you will be reminded of how God used them to mold you.

Sometimes the molding process takes time. God may show us something, but we don't react to what we have witnessed for a while. Maybe we didn't see the whole picture right away, or maybe we were too scared to make changes immediately. No matter the reason, the most important part is that we eventually apply these life lessons to our lives.

Anxiety weighs down the heart, but a kind word cheers it up. (Proverbs 12:25 NIV)

I try to be an optimistic person. Yes, I'm one of those happy, bubbly women who drive others crazy. But I take Proverbs 12:25 to heart. I want to encourage those around me. I want to help make their day a little brighter. How many of you have had someone mention something about your hair, outfit, or smile? It builds you up on the inside. I'm not talking about boasting, just little comments here or there to show encouragement to others. I believe all Christians should be optimistic, seeing the glass half full instead of half empty. What do you think? Agree or disagree?

I know, I know: we can't be happy-go-lucky all the time. We all have our moments of low times. But that's when it's even more important that someone else is there to lift us up.

Last year at work, I decided that things were a little gloomy, so I purchased some cute blank cards and began to write personal letters to people in the building. I tried to write two to three cards per day for a couple of weeks. Before I knew it, I was filled with so much joy because I shared my joy with others. It was inspiring and encouraging. I had a few coworkers come talk to me about personal struggles they were experiencing. I prayed with them and led them to scriptures of encouragement. If I had never taken the initiative to write the cards, I would never had found out about their struggles. It just took a few minutes each day, and the results were worth the time invested.

One of my most favorite sayings I see it all over Facebook, is, "You never know the trials that people are facing, so just be nice." How true is this statement? And how are you doing in this category? Do you struggle with always seeing the class half empty or completely empty? Are the struggles of this life holding you down? Be reminded that your children see everything you do and hear everything you say. Show them you have a reason to be happy. There is always hope when Jesus is near, and He promises to never leave us or forsake us!

In this world we will experience sorrow, pain, discouragement, and other not-so-great days. In this life, we must face death, loss of friendships, and even changes God calls us to that may cause us to mourn. So how do we deal with these situations in a healthy manner?

First of all, remember you are in a season of life. It's okay to feel what you are feeling. Remember you are human. No matter how much you fight it, you live in a world with Satan as it's prince. The pain and discouragement you feel our from him. God has a remedy for these times. He is the remedy. Satan may be the prince of this world, but God is the King of it all!

Sorrow comes in many different forms. We mourn the loss of friendships, loved ones who have left this world, and sometimes even our own personal loss. During these moments, you must have a plan in place to overcome. This will take time. In fact, rushing the healing process is not the way to go. *Sorr*ow needs time to heal. Processes take time!

Joy and sorrow go hand in hand. Those who inspire us most are those whom we will grieve for most once they are gone. These times have been extremely hard for me. Here are some examples of how I have dealt with sorrow.

1. Praise God daily for placing this person in my life.
2. Journal about my feelings, emotions, and thoughts. Then read my writings as a prayer back to God.
3. Share my feelings with close friends and family. I have found it is better to be an open book, releasing my pain, than a closed book, holding it all in and trying to deal with it on my own.
   a. This takes a lot of courage, trust, and faith in the people you open up to. It only takes one or two close friends. This may just be your spouse. And that is okay.
   b. As a friend to a friend, if someone ever confides in you, *do not* reveal these truths to anyone. Be quick to listen and slow to speak. Most of the time, we simply need to listen, cry together, give a hug, and then pray it out.

Who do is someone you have lost to death but you wish you could have one more day with them? Why do you think you miss this person so much? If you could talk to them, what would you want to talk to them about? Write your response as if they were here with you today. Reread what you have written. This person was very valuable to you! Can you depict why?

This week, call, write a letter, or meet with someone who has inspired you over the years. Let people know you appreciate them!

Day 2: Mapping God's Word

Hebrews 10: 23 - 24

Write It Down and Map It Out

Define Words, Thesaurus, and Commentaries

Summary

Apply It to Your Life

Pray It Back to God

Day 3: Mapping God's Word

Galatians 6:2

Write It Down and Map It Out

Define Words, Thesaurus, and Commentaries

Summary

Apply It to Your Life

Pray It Back to God

Day 4: Mapping God's Word

1 Peter 4: 8 - 10

Write It Down and Map It Out

Define Words, Thesaurus, and Commentaries

Summary

Apply It to Your Life

Pray It Back to God

CHAPTER 1 THRU 7 MEMORY VERSES

Rewrite your memory verses from previous chapters below. Pick one of the verses you mapped this week to memorize. Rewrite the verse you have chosen below in chapter 7's section.

Chapter 1 memory verse:
Chapter 2 memory verse: Hebrews 11:23
Chapter 3 memory verse:
Chapter 4 memory verse: Ruth 1:16

Chapter 5 memory verse:

Chapter 6 memory verse: 2 Corinthians 11:3

Chapter 7 memory verse:

CHAPTER 7 REVIEW

Day 1: Inspired by others

Choose one of the people who have inspired you over the years. Write below what you would like to share with your group about this amazing person. Or look back on this week's lesson to be ready to share about him or her.

Are you an encourager to those around you? Is this something that comes naturally, or something that you have to work at? What methods of encouragement have you used in the past that have produced good fruits?

Day 2 thru 4: Mapping God's Word

Pick one of the verses from this week to share with your class. Pick the verse that spoke the most to you. Look back over your map for this verse. Be prepared to share how you have applied or plan on applying this verse to your life.

Chapter 8

Mary and Martha

As Jesus and his disciples were on their way, he came to a village where a woman named Martha opened her home to him. She had a sister Mary, who sat at the Lord's feet listening to what he said. (Luke 10:38–39 NIV)

Mary and Martha

Orderly desire and spiritual desire

Mary and Martha, both sisters to Lazarus, were two very different women. They both held characteristics of great women. They each had an approach of their own. Martha was the orderly sister. She kept the house nice, clean, and ready for visitors. Mary was more of a laid-back sort of woman. She loved to learn about things—specifically Jesus. Jesus was a close family friend, along with being her Savior. She wanted to learn and grow closer to Him every chance she got. I'm sure she helped Martha when Martha asked her to help. However, on this specific visit Mary wanted to spend time with Jesus. She knew His time with her was short. How did Jesus respond to these two women? Both having excellent reasons for their actions and characters.

Day 1

- Luke 10: 38 – 42 Both girls sit at Jesus' feet, Jesus rebukes Martha
  - o Whose home were Jesus and his disciples invited?____________________
  - o Verse 39: What did Mary do while Jesus was in the home?

- Verse 40: How did Martha react to Mary's actions?

    - What do you think of Martha's reaction to Mary? How would you have felt if you were Martha?

    - How do you think Mary felt about Martha's reaction? If you were Mary, what would your response be?

    - Do both of these women have a legitimate excuse for their behaviors? Explain your reasoning.

- Verse 41 - 42: Jesus' reaction to Martha's question:
    - Verse 41: Jesus responds by saying Martha's name twice…why do you think he said her name 2 times? Is this significant?

    - Verse 41: Jesus then tells her 'you are worried and upset about many things'
        - How well did Jesus know Martha? ______________________________
        - What do you think He meant by his comment to her?

- Have you ever been in a situation where you put more time and effort into the preparation, then missed out on opportunities of growth around you? Explain.

- Verse 42: Jesus reminds Martha of what's important
  - What one thing did Jesus tell Martha was needed at this moment in time? ____________________
  - Basically, He told Martha—Mary is right, and you are wrong. How easy is that for you? When you are called out for your actions being wrong? Do you accept this easily? Or is it more difficult for you? Explain.

Day 2

- What lesson did you learn from yesterday's passage?
  - True hospitality is a gift we share with others. Do you like to invite other people into your home? If not, why not? If so, what is on your list of 'to-do's' before your company arrives?

  - If you knew of someone that needed a place of shelter immediately, would you open your home to them? No matter who they were? No matter how clean your home was? Explain.

- Comparing ourselves to others is NOT the answer. Martha was upset with Mary because Mary did not share the same desires as herself. That doesn't make Mary's actions wrong; nor does it make Martha's actions wrong. They were both seeing the situation from different perspectives.
  - Martha became extremely anxious when she realized Mary was not helping her. She quickly jumped to a conclusion that Mary should be doing the same as herself. What is wrong with this thinking?
  - How about you? Do you assume that others should see things the same way you see them? What sort of feelings has this stirred up inside you? Good or not so good results?
  - SOMETHING TO THINK ABOUT: When we are quick to judge others, we are only seeing a snapshot of their life. Decisions they are making at that split moment. How could our perceptions change if we knew more about this individual? Do you have a life example that could be used here?

Day 3

- Continue learning from this week's passage?
  - When we are frustrated with our circumstances, take it straight to the boss—Jesus! Martha felt so admit about her feelings that she took her concern straight to Jesus. Sounds pretty bold to me. First, she was a woman. Second, all the disciples were also in the house. Third, she was angry. So her words were not thought through before she spoke them.

- Do have an example of a time in your life where you went off on God? Be honest. We are all human. What were the circumstances?

- Scripture does not continue on to let us know Martha's reaction to Jesus' response. If you were Martha, what would you have done?

- Something to consider. When we have our moments of frustration and/or anger that we vent to God, we should ask God to forgive us our short comings. He is faithful! He will forgive you. And then learn from these situations about us, our limitations, and how we should react in the future. Agree? Disagree?

- <u>We can tell Jesus anything!</u> Jesus did not respond to Martha with harsh words or rebuke her for her frustrations. He listened to Martha right where she was and responded to her in love.
  - Just as Jesus responded to Martha, He will respond to you. Jesus doesn't get offended when we come to Him with our frustrations. I love this!! He speaks to us, with love, encourages us to change our approach, and then moves on. There is value in this knowledge! He is an example of the perfect friend. How are you doing in this area of your life? Do you jump on the bandwagon of gossip? Encouraging others by feeding into their anger and frustrations? Or do you bring peace? Seek God about your relationships, and how you can better handle them.

Day 4

- John 11: 1 – 4 Lazarus, Mary and Martha's brother, has died
    - When Jesus heard that Lazarus was dead, what was His response?
- John 11: 5 – 7 Jesus loved this family
    - Why does scripture tell us that Jesus loved this family, but then proceeds to say He staid where He was 2 more days?
- John 11: 7 – 16 Pay attention disciples!
    - Oh disciples, they missed so much of Jesus teachings. What was Jesus trying to tell his disciples, but they missed it.
    - Verse 16: What did Thomas mean by "that we may die with him"?
- John 11: 17 – 27 Martha's reaction to Jesus
    - Describe how Martha reacted to Jesus' visit:

- John 11: 28 – 35 Mary's reaction to Jesus
  - Describe how Mary reacted to Jesus' visit:
  - Jesus had compassion for the loss of Lazarus. He was moved by the sorrow around him. What does this tell us about Jesus?
- John 11: 36 - 45
  - Describe the scene portrayed here. Why do you think Jesus raised Lazarus from the dead?

Here is a little bit about Mary and Martha...

Who are you more like, Mary or Martha? I wish I could say I was more like Mary, but I'm more like Martha. I'm a fixer, cleaner, and "put everything where it belongs" kind of woman. Yes, I have my moments like Mary. I want to learn more and more about God and dig into His Word. But deep down, I'm a Martha through and through.

The scriptures tell us that Mary and Martha both begin at Jesus's feet. Martha was not against Jesus; she is the one who rushes to meet Him on the road toward her home after Lazarus's death. She begins by scolding Jesus, asking Him why He had not come. But she proves her belief in that she tells Jesus all He has to do is say the word, and her brother will come alive. She knew Him, trusted Him, and believed in Him.

Mary is much more passive, but she wanted to be close to Jesus. She anoints His feet with costly oils. She uses her hair to clean his feet. She becomes completely humble before Him. Her form of worship was humble and soothing love. The scriptures do not tell us whether she ever helped Martha, but knowing the women's roles in this time period, I would venture to guess she did help her. Yet when Jesus was around, she focused all her attention on Him.

Both of these women loved Jesus; they simply showed it in two different ways. Jesus loved them both equally. Even though they showed Him love in different ways, He showed that He loved and appreciated them both.

But we have that one moment when Martha complained to Jesus about Mary. Oh, boy, here we go … We Marthas always are complaining about those Marys sitting and twiddling their thumbs. Actually, Jesus rebuked Martha and said (in my words of course), "Be still, woman. Mary is okay to sit and listen. In fact, you should take a moment to listen to my words as well. Stop worrying about everything being just right. Sit and listen to me, for what I have to say will change your life." Ouch—Martha got schooled by Jesus! And I believe we Marthas need to listen and abide by Jesus's words. Stop and take time to be with Him. It's okay if everything is not in its place. It's more important to spend time with God than to make sure the toilet paper is facing the right way.

Here is what can we learn from Mary and Martha.

1. Jesus **appreciated** and **loved** them both very much.

    Now Jesus loved Martha and her sister and Lazarus. (John 11:5)

2. Mary teaches us **to be still and listen** to Jesus's Words.

    And she had a sister called Mary, who sat at the Lord's feet listening to his teaching. (Luke 10:39)

3. Martha was always **prepared to welcome and feed** Jesus into her home.

    Now as they went on their way, Jesus entered a village. And a woman named Martha welcomed him into her house. (Luke 10:38)

CHAPTER 1 THRU 8 MEMORY VERSES

Rewrite your memory verses from previous chapters below. I have given you your memory verse for chapter 8. Chose which translation you would prefer to use for this verse. Copy it below! Happy memorizing!

Chapter 1 memory verse:
Chapter 2 memory verse: Hebrews 11:23
Chapter 3 memory verse:
Chapter 4 memory verse: Ruth 1:16

Chapter 5 memory verse:
Chapter 6 memory verse: 2 Corinthians 11:3
Chapter 7 memory verse:
Chapter 8 memory verse: Luke 10:41-42

CHAPTER 8 REVIEW

Mary and Martha

1. Did our character this week have a relationship with God? If so, describe that relationship. Include any changes that may have occurred with this relationship.

2. Describe this woman's character. What can we learn from her about faith, love, marriage, being a mother, grief, strength, perseverance, and more.

3. List an example of how this woman handled a specific struggle. Pay attention to details. These details help teach us right steps verses wrong steps to take.

4. What can we learn about being a wife or mother from this woman's story?

Chapter 9

Super Mom

Start children off in the way they should go, and even when they
are old they will not turn from it. (Proverbs 22:6 NIV)

Day 1: Super Mom

It's hard to be a good mom. We must be able to balance multiple hats at the same time: nurse, cook, wife, disciplinarian, janitor … the list goes on. How do we balance all these hats plus keep our own sanity? Does God have a plan in place to make our jobs easier? Is it even possible to be a good mom? The answer is yes to all of these questions. God has a plan for each of us. We all walk different paths of life laid out before us, but we all share the desire to be good Godly women and mothers. Together, we will unlock the truth about being a good Christian mother.

I am a working mom of three beautiful children: Kaytlin, nineteen; Noah, sevententeen; and Caleb, thirteen. I teach seventh grade science at a local public school. I have been teaching for twenty years. I am one of those drill sergeant moms. The kids and I share chores in the home, mainly laundry and dishes. My husband is a full-time farmer. How much assistance I get at home is dependent upon what he's doing with the farm; there are days that I feel like a single parent. Here's my list of jobs for the past twenty-four hours.

- Teacher (full time at school)
- Teacher (at home for my kids' homework)
- Housekeeper (laundry, cleaning, picking up, etc.)
- Chef
- Counselor (for my daughter and her friends)
- Secretary (for my husband's business)
- Dog groomer
- Traffic operator (Keeping track of where all my family members are located at all times)
- Anger manager (for my children—and myself)
- Disciplinarian (yes, you will eat what I made for dinner, like it or not!)
- Loving wife (well, okay, not always the loving part)
- Keeper of the family schedule (where is everyone, and what time do people have to be there?)

Anyone feeling slightly stressed yet? We all live busy lives, eagerly seeking out jobs to keep us busy … Yeah, right. More like wishing we could hire our own personal housekeepers, chefs, and massage therapists. Believe it or not, God has equipped you for such a time as this! Thinking about all these job titles can take away all hope from ever getting a good night's sleep or making it through one week without saying the word "Timeout." But let me give you hope. Even if you go to bed tired and wake up tired, these are the days of your life—days that will give meaning and value to your life. God has equipped you for such a time as this.

Don't believe the lies of Satan. You were made for this. God has given you these children because He knows you are the best mother for these children. You can do this! Satan wants you to look at the list of jobs, become discouraged, and give in to negative thinking. And mamas, it is so easy for us to do just that. Satan knows he has us when we begin to devalue ourselves. God did not give you children to make your life miserable. He gave you children to give your life enjoyment. Believe it!

The world has a misconception of mothers. They put us in a category that makes us believe we are equal to our husbands, capable of doing everything a man can do. Is this biblical? Did God create man and woman equal? Give your opinion below. Back up your answer with scripture!

Let's evaluate the situation. God created you to be a woman capable of being a great mom. What's holding you back from believing this? What to-do list item causes you the most stress? Make a list for yourself of all the job titles you held in the past twenty-four hours.

Look back over your list and determine what items can wait. You may have things on your list that are a must. These are things that you must do daily for the health and well-being of your family. Other things on your list may not be as important. Oh, I know: to you they are all important. But when you look at the bigger picture, the health and well-being of your family, they don't line up. What we do daily is our choice! Make wise choices.

Now, I also understand that we have moments in our lives when there are items placed on our to-do list we didn't intend: sickness, emotional struggles, and baggage our children (and we ourselves) may carry from outside relationships. Listen to me clearly: God knows all things. He knows what needs to be done for your children's well-being. He is your first response when deciding the value of a to-do list. Seek His will above all others. Pray, listen, read His Word, and be alert to all the signs He places around you each and every day.

Be ready to share with your group this week. Be open and honest about your struggles. Your group should be a safe place to be you—the true you. We all have things we struggle with. Be respectful of other women's struggles too. Be ready with words to uplift, encourage, and bring strength. Cry together, laugh together, and grow together.

Day 2: Mapping God's Word

Proverbs 22:6

Write It Down and Map It Out

Define Words, Thesaurus, and Commentaries

Summary

Apply It to Your Life

Pray It Back to God

Day 3: Mapping God's Word

Romans 8:28

Write It Down and Map It Out

Define Words, Thesaurus, and Commentaries

Summary

Apply It to Your Life

Pray It Back to God

Day 4: Mapping God's Word

Isaiah 40:29

Write It Down and Map It Out

Define Words, Thesaurus, and Commentaries

Summary

Apply It to Your Life

Pray It Back to God

CHAPTER 1 THRU 9 MEMORY VERSES

Rewrite your memory verses from the previous chapters below. Pick one of the verses you mapped this week to memorize. Rewrite the verse you have chosen below in chapter 9's section.

Chapter 1 memory verse:
Chapter 2 memory verse: Hebrews 11:23
Chapter 3 memory verse:
Chapter 4 memory verse: Ruth 1:16

Chapter 5 memory verse:

Chapter 6 memory verse: 2 Corinthians 11:3

Chapter 7 memory verse:

Chapter 8 memory verse: Luke 10: 41 - 42

Chapter 9 memory verse:

CHAPTER 9 REVIEW

Day 1: Super Mom

How can we change the way we see our to-do list as moms? Is there a method you use that helps you get through each day or week without driving yourself crazy?

Which daily or weekly jobs cause you the most stress in completing? Why do you think this is so?

Pick one job that you do weekly. Every time you begin working on this job, thank God for blessing you with your family. Change your approach to the work. Be thankful!

If you are a veteran mom in your group, what are words of wisdom you share with your group for encouragement, whether it was something you learned through mistakes or something you did right? Either way, young moms needs our encouragement to get through!

Day 2 thru 4: Mapping God's Word

Pick one of the verses from this week to share with your class. Pick the verse that spoke the most to you. Look back over your map for this verse. Be prepared to share how you have applied or plan on applying this verse to your life.

Chapter 10

Sarah

And by faith even Sarah, who was past the childbearing age, was enabled to bear children because she considered him faithful who had made the promise. (Hebrews 11:11 NIV)

Sarah

The Virtue of Patience

Look up the scriptures below about Sarah, Abraham's wife. She had to endure much patience in her life. She didn't always make the right decisions; she failed just like we all do. We can learn a lot from Sarah about patience and enduring the consequences of our choices. You may want to keep notes about Sarah's actions, mistakes, blessings, and failures—whatever you find in the scriptures below. Remember that we are going to use these lessons for ourselves. Yes, Abraham had two wives. None of us may be able to relate to that situation, but we can relate her circumstances to the same or similar circumstances in our lives. What choices did she make? What were the consequences or blessings from those choices?

Day 1

Today we will begin in Genesis, this is where we meet Sarah. She was known as Sarai at this time. God changes her name to Sarah later in her life. As you read the verses, complete the questions that follow.

- Genesis 11: 29 – 32: Sarai is barren
  - o Who did Sarai marry? _______________

- Verse 30 tells us something extremely important about Sarai. What does God reveal about her? ______________________________
  - **What does this mean?**

- Terah, Abram's father, begins a journey with Abram, Sarai, and Lot (Abram's nephew). They set out for ____________________________, but they end up stopping in _________.
  - **We find that Abram's father dies here. Abram's family must have been somewhat close to one another.**
- Sarai's name meant 'contentious'. Define contentious:

- Abram's name means 'Father'. How ironic! His wife could have no children. How do you think this made Sarai feel? Explain your answer.

FYI: Abram's family were idol worshipers (Joshua 24:2). Abram left Ur because God had called him to leave his father's land to get away from the idol worshipers (Acts 7:2-4). In Genesis 12:1 – 3, we learn what God said to Abram. This promise was now not only for Abram, but was also a promise to Sarai his wife.

- Genesis 12:4 – 20: Abram and Sarai's lie
  - Abram obeyed God. He took his wife, Sarai, and his nephew, Lot, and left Haran and moved to the land of ____________________________. Has he continued his journey, he ended up in Egypt. Why?

- Before entering Egypt, Abram asked Sarai to lie and say she was his sister. Why did he ask her to lie? Why do you think she obeyed her husband?

- What happened to Pharaoh because of this Abram's lie? Do you think this was an act of God? If so why? If not, why not?

Day 2

- Genesis 15:1 – 6: Abram is promised children
  - Abram had just defeated an army of 5 kings working together. He was afraid for his life. What does God promise Abram in a vision?

  - The king of Sodom had offered Abram great reward, but he didn't take it. God knew Abram needed to know God had his back. But in verses 2 – 3 Abram ask God for decedents. Abram knew when he married Sarai she was barren. This question he presented to God was not only bold, but an open honesty before the Lord. Abram list one man as the heir to his house. What was this man's name? ______________________________
    - This man was Abram's chief assistant, his right-hand man. He was a great man, but not a decedent of Abrams.
  - What promise does God give Abram (and Sarai)?

  - God confirmed His promise with an illustration. What illustration did he lay out for Abram?

- Abram's response to God's confirmation of his promise in bearing his own biological children is priceless. Read verse 6 again along with the following New Testament verses.
  - Romans 4:1-3
  - Romans 4:19-24
  - Galatians 3:5-7
    - According to these verses, how was Abram's faith in God?
- How does this knowledge of Abram reflect on his wife Sarai? His faith cannot make her righteous. But how can Abram's faith help Sarai become faithful to God?

Day 3

- Genesis 16:1 – 12: Sarai and Hagar
  - Sarai tries to take matters into her own hands here. Who was Hagar?______________
  - Sarai pleads with Abram to sleep with Hagar. This is very similar to a surrogate mother arrangement. Even in these times, if Hagar were to bear a child. The child would have been considered Abram's and Sarai's.
    - It had been 10 years since God had made the promise to Abram. God had not told Abram or Sarai that Hagar was a part of this promise. However, Abram submitted to Sarai's request. Why do you think they both seen this as an OK think to do?
  - When Hagar became pregnant, it was as if Sarai became convinced that she was the problem. No children had been born because she was barren.

- Verse 5: How did Hagar react to this pregnancy?
- Read verses 5 – 6. How did Sarai handle this pregnancy? Where did she place the blame? What did she want Abram to do?
- In verse 6, Abram gives Sarai the power over Hagar. Do you feel this was a good move on Abram's part, or a bad move? Explain your reasoning.

- Genesis 17: 15 – 22: Abraham is promised Isaac
  - God changes Sarai's name to Sarah. He adds more detail to his original promise for Abram. What is Sarah promised (verse 16)?
  - What was Abraham's reaction to God's promise for Sarah? He ____________________. Read Romans 4:17 – 21. How are these verses relevant to Abraham's situation?
  - God tells Abraham to name his son Isaac. Do you know what the name Isaac means? ________________ At this point God even gives Abraham a due date, how long will Abraham have to wait?

- Genesis 18: 1 – 16: Sarah laughs
    - o With the visit of these 3 men, Sarah over hears a conversation. She laughs. Why do you think she laughed?
    - o When Abraham approached Sarah about the situation, she denied laughing. But Abraham new she had laughed. How do you think he knew?

Day 4

- Genesis 20:1 – 18: Abraham and Sarah lie again
    - o Abraham and Sarah venture back into the same sin they had dealt with before (Genesis 12). Instead of trusting God to keep his family safe, he devoted a plan to do it himself. But his plan fails completely. Explain the what happens this time when he lies and says Sarah is his wife:
    - o Did God abandon Abraham or Sarah because of their sin? _____ What excuse did Abraham give Ahimelech for his deception?
    - o What was Ahimelech's response? Does this surprise you?

- Genesis 21:1 – 14: Sarah's jealousy
  - How old was Abraham when Isaac was born? ______________ Did God full fill His promise to Abraham? Was Isaac born one year from God's promise?
  - What happens between Isaac and Ishmael?
  - How does God handle this situation with Abraham?
  - What happens to Ishmael and his mother? This was part of God's plan. Why do you think God had Abraham do this?
- Genesis 23: 1 – 2: Sarah dies
  - How old was Sarah when she died? ________________

Here is a little bit about Sarah...

Abraham's wife, Sarah, certainly had her moments as a wife and mother. Her list of struggles may sound similar to some of ours. She and her husband struggled with fear. Fear that God would not keep His promises. Fear they would never have a child. These fears led to lying and deception. Sarah tried to take control of her own situation. She tried to fix her and her husband's problem all on her own. Interesting, isn't it? We are quick to judge Sarah for jumping ahead of God and plowing a new road to children. Yet how many of us in our own lives do the same thing? We see a desire, decide which way to get us there, take it, and all the while know that our actions were never condoned by God. Then we seem surprised when God says, "Hey, what are you doing?" We could very easily throw Abraham under the bus and accuse him of following along with Sarah's plan. He should have known not to sleep with Hagar. He should have been the one to correct this mistake before it ever happened. Oh, come on, now. We all know God doesn't want us to put our failures off on someone else. Abraham had his own punishments from these choices, and Sarah had her own punishments. She dealt with jealousy her whole life. Poor Hagar; Sarah treated her so poorly. With all these mistakes, does Sarah's life have any lesson for us? What can we learn from her story?

God forgave Sarah. God kept his promises to her. She was full of joy. With all she endured, scripture says she was full of joy! Ladies, use Sarah's life as an example: failures may occur, but God is faithful. He will forgive you, love you through it, keep His promises to you, and give you joy!

1. Sarah was **faithful** to her husband.

   Like Sarah, who obeyed Abraham and called him her lord. (1 Peter 3:6a NIV)

2. Sarah **believed** in God and held **true** to His promises.

   By faith Sarah, herself received power to conceive, even when she was past the age, since she considered him faithful who had promised. (Hebrew 11:11 ESV)

3. Sarah had the **joy** of the Lord.

> Sarah said, "God has made me laughter, and everyone who hears about this will laugh with me." And she added "Who would have said to Abraham that Sarah would nurse children? Yet I have borne him a son in his old age." (Genesis 21:6–7)

CHAPTER 1 THRU 10 MEMORY VERSES

Rewrite your memory verses from previous chapters below. I have given you your memory verse for chapter 10. Chose which translation you would prefer to use for this verse. Copy it below! Happy memorizing!

Chapter 1 memory verse:
Chapter 2 memory verse: Hebrews 11:23
Chapter 3 memory verse:
Chapter 4 memory verse: Ruth 1:16

Chapter 5 memory verse:
Chapter 6 memory verse: 2 Corinthians 11:3
Chapter 7 memory verse:
Chapter 8 memory verse: Luke 10: 41 - 42

Chapter 9 memory verse:
Chapter 10 memory verse: Hebrews 11:11

CHAPTER 6 REVIEW

Sarah

1. Did our character this week have a relationship with God? If so, describe that relationship. Include any changes that may have occurred with this relationship.

2. Describe this woman's character. What can we learn from her about faith, love, marriage, being a mother, grief, strength, perseverance, and more.

3. List an example of how this woman handled a specific struggle. Pay attention to details. These details help teach us right steps verses wrong steps to take.

4. What can we learn about being a wife or mother from this woman's story?

Chapter 11

Trust in God

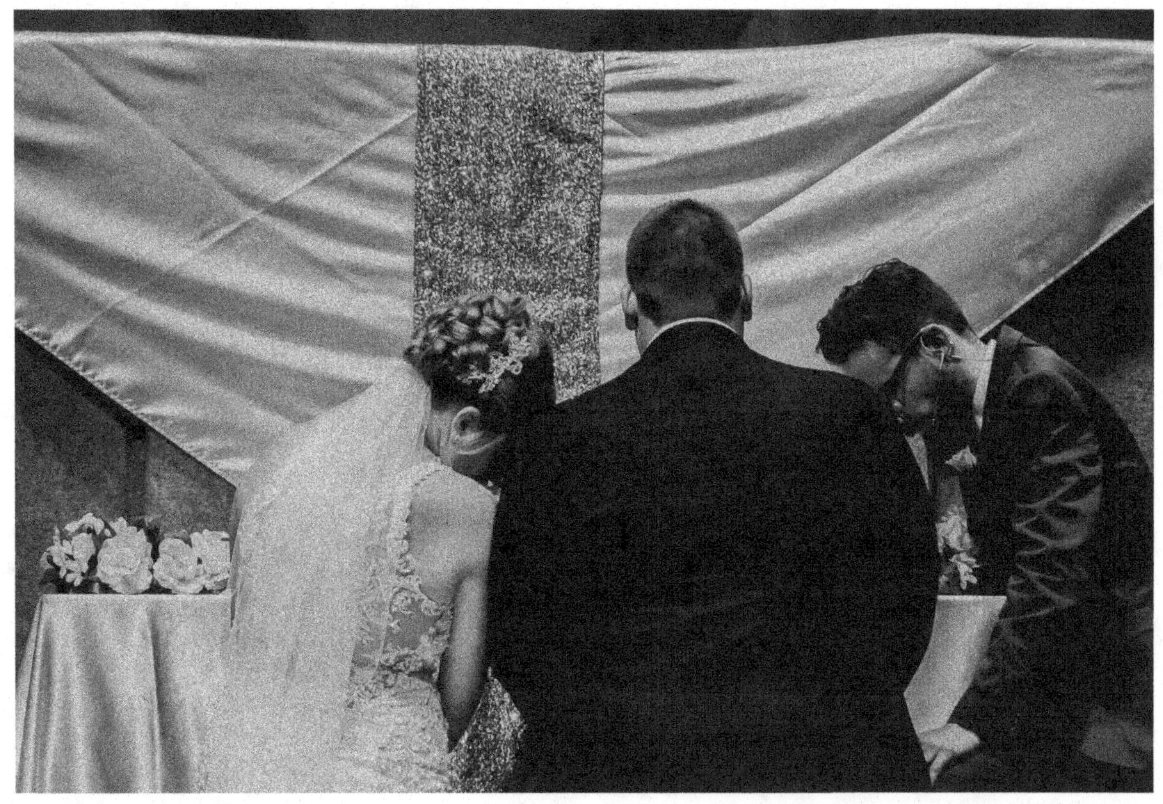

Wives submit to your own husbands as you do to the Lord. For the husband is the head of the wife as Christ is the head of the church, his body, of which he is the Savior. (Ephesians 5:22–23 NIV)

Day 1: Trust God

Today we are going to start by talking about our husbands. How many of us appreciate our husbands? Have you ever sat down and made a list of all the wonderful things your husband does for your family? Well, take a moment to consider this thought. Make a list in the space below:

Okay, now grab a few different colored highlighters or colored pencils. Let's discuss your list. The first role of a Godly husband is leadership. Select a color and shade over all the things on your list that include leadership skills or roles.

Leadership = Influence family by biblical teachings
Reference: 1 Corinthians 11:3

Another role of our husbands is to provide and protect the family. Select another color to shade things on your list that include providing and protection.

Provide and protect = Emotionally, financially, physically, and spiritually
Reference: 1 Timothy 5:6; 1 Peter 3:7

A husband should also be compassionate with you, his wife. Choose another color to shade this concept from your list above.

Compassionate = Putting the needs of others above his own
References: Ephesians 5:22–23; Genesis 2:20–24

Whew! How was that? If you're like me, you had to add to the list as I asked you to shade. I kept thinking of more things my husband does for me and our family. After completing this exercise, you will either:

A. appreciate your husband more and more for all he does for your family, or
B. see gaps or holes where your husband struggles to lead your family according to God's Word.

For all you (A) women, take a moment to thank God for the man He has given you. You are one lucky woman. Also, take some time this week to show your husband how much you appreciate him. Men need encouraged just as much as we do. Plus, remember there is no perfect man except Jesus. Expect your man to fail, because he will. Simply keep loving him and continue to encourage him to seek God. Then support him as he strives to be a man of God.

For all you (B) women, take the time to praise God for your man. He may not have it all together, but he needs your support. Being the leader of a family is an extremely tough job and high calling. Be an encourager, not a discourager. Let him know you love him right where he is. Encourage him to seek out other Christian men as fellow counselors and advisers. Most churches have groups of men who meet to support and help each other grow. Let your man know he is capable of this high calling. Never discourage him. Be his biggest supporter!

All of us women need to pray for and with our husbands. They need to know we are here as their helpmates. We are ready to walk by their sides through thick and thin. God has called us to follow our husbands' leadership, so that is what we will do!

Disclaimer: This does not give your husband permission to mistreat you in any way, shape, or form. He is to treat you as Christ treats the Church. Christ gave His live for the Church. If you fear for your safety or the safety of your children, seek help. Talk to the leader of your group, a pastor, or a trusting friend. No woman or man deserves to be in an abusive relationship!

This week, take time out of your schedule to show appreciation for your husband. Write him a love letter, make him his favorite meal, or turn up the heat in the bedroom (or wherever). He is a gift from God. Let him know you appreciate him.

What will you vow to do for your husband this week?

After you follow through with your vow above, write a reflection about what you did. How did your husband react? How did you feel afterward about yourself and about your husband?

Do you think this is something you could do more often? Explain why or why not.

This discussion of husbands can sometimes lead to jealousy. Just like Sarah, we can easily become jealous of others. Usually the qualities our husbands struggle with, or lack, are the first things we see in other women's husbands. If our own husband is not as affectionate as we'd like, we become jealous when we see our friend's or acquaintance's spouse show affection toward his wife. Satan enters our mind, and we think to ourselves, "I wish my husband would do that!" Some women even enter a fantasy world where they get more and more upset at their own spouse. However, he never did anything wrong, so he has no idea what has caused you to be so upset with him. Without even trying, you have caused problems in your marriage because of Satan's mind interpretations.

We can react like Sarah and speak in anger. Or we can talk to God, search His Word, and approach our husbands with love. I believe that we need to talk to our husbands about struggles like these, but not until we talk to God about them. After conversing with God (talking and listening), we may realize that we need to refocus ourselves and appreciate our husband for who he is. God gave you your husband because He knew the two of you were best together. When you spend your time dwelling on rages of jealousy, you miss out on what makes your husband just right for you. You may also find that all those great qualities you see in other spouses are qualities God is calling you to show your husband. Men typically respond to women who show honor and appreciation toward them. How long has it been since you have purposefully set out to show your man that you appreciate him? You may be surprised how much happier you whole relationship will be if you give him the adoration and honor you are seeking him to give you.

There is one thing that can help your marriage grow in statute, trust, love, and affection, and that is Jesus Christ. As head of your household, your husband is called to lead your family in the ways of the Lord. As we have previously discussed, that is an extremely tough job. As his wife, you are called to stand by your husband with love and support. Let's be honest: men and women see things differently on so many levels. With this being true, we women sometimes feel that we know what's best in all situations in which we may find our families. We want to lead the husband to the truth, but that's not our job. So here's the deal: you must first trust that God loves you and wants what is best for you. Second, you must trust that your husband also loves you and wants what is best for you and your family. Third, together you must seek God. The key word in this statement is *together*. Together, fall on your knees before God and ask Him to direct your path. Trust God that He knows what He is doing (read Jeremiah 29:11–13). Then trust your husband to follow God's will for your family.

See the key word in there? Trust. No marriage is successful without this little word that means so much! Trusting your husband to lead you and your children is so much easier when God is at the center of your marriage.

How is our relationship with God related to your relationship with your husband?

In what areas have you seen your husband follow God's will, where your family has been blessed? (Don't feel bad if you have nothing to put here … yet! You will, by faith. Keep believing and trusting.)

Make a list of ways you can help support your husband as he seeks God to make decisions for your family.

Day 2: Mapping God's Word

Ephesians 5:22 - 23

Write It Down and Map It Out

Define Words, Thesaurus, and Commentaries

Summary

Apply It to Your Life

Pray It Back to God

Day 3: Mapping God's Word

John 13: 34 - 35

Write It Down and Map It Out

Define Words, Thesaurus, and Commentaries

Summary

Apply It to Your Life

Pray It Back to God

Day 4: Mapping God's Word

1 Corinthians 11:3

Write It Down and Map It Out

Define Words, Thesaurus, and Commentaries

Summary

Apply It to Your Life

Pray It Back to God

CHAPTER 1 THRU 11 MEMORY VERSES

Rewrite your memory verses from the previous chapters below. Pick one of the verses you mapped this week to memorize. Rewrite the verse you have chosen below in chapter 11's section.

Chapter 1 memory verse:
Chapter 2 memory verse: Hebrews 11:23
Chapter 3 memory verse:
Chapter 4 memory verse: Ruth 1:16

Chapter 5 memory verse:
Chapter 6 memory verse: 2 Corinthians 11:3
Chapter 7 memory verse:
Chapter 8 memory verse: Luke 10: 41 - 42

Chapter 9 memory verse:
Chapter 10 memory verse: Hebrews 11:11
Chapter 11 memory verse:

CHAPTER 11 REVIEW

Day 1: Trusting God

If you could pick one thing to brag about your husband, what would it be?

Is there an area or role that your husband struggles with? If so, seek God in prayer about this situation. It could be very easy to become negative about your man, but God calls us to speak words to uplift (1 Thessalonians 5:11). You may want to write your prayer, but not in this book. Write your prayer in a separate prayer journal. It is something that you can use to talk to God throughout the days to come. Something to be kept between you and God alone.

Briefly describe what you did for your hubby this week. Your idea may encourage someone else to give it a try.

Day 3 and 4: Mapping God's Word

Pick one of the verses from this week to share with your class. Pick the verse that spoke the most to you. Look back over your map for this verse. Be prepared to share how you have applied or plan on applying this verse to your life.

Chapter 12

Hagar

Now Sarai, Abram's wife, had borne him no children. She had a female Egyptian slave named Hagar. (Genesis 16:1 NIV)

Hagar

The Virtue of Endurance

Look up the scriptures below about Hagar, Sarai's handmaiden and mother of Ishmael (Israel). Hagar was never able to make many decisions on her own when living under Abram's tent; she was under Sarai's control. Without Sarai's pushing, Hagar may have never had Ishmael. Having Ishmael changed Hagar's life. Sarai always treated Hagar sharply because of her jealousy. Hagar loved Ishmael despite Sarai's constant looks and angry commands. Living under Abram's tent did teach Hagar something, the most important thing: God loved her and created her and her son for a purpose. It is with this hope that she endured so much hatred and mistreatment. God saw her hope, and with that hope she learned to endure.

Day 1

Today we will begin in Genesis. This is where Hagar and Sari first meet one another. Neither woman knew how their lives would become so tangled in a mess created by the drive of the flesh. The name Hagar means "fugitive" or "immigrant." So fitting for her story.

- Genesis 12: 4 -20

- Remember the story of Sarai and Abram lying to the Egyptians out of fear? Sarai claimed to be Abram's sister and was taken in by Pharaoh as part of his harem. Pharaoh rewarded Abram with camels, sheep, cattle, donkeys, and servants. It is not for certain, but believed that this is how Hagar, an Egyptian slave, became part of Abram and Sarai's workers.
    - Don't you find it ironic that Hagar's relationship with Sarai started from a lie. Interesting…

- Genesis 16: 1 – 6 Egyptian slave
    - What did Sarai suggest to Abram about Hagar?
        - Did she have to try to convince Abram to do this, or did he quickly volunteer?

    - Verse 4: Once Hagar knew she was pregnant; how did Sarai feel towards her?

Day 2

- Genesis 16: 7 – 16 God talks to Hagar
    - Hagar, a pregnant woman in a foreign land, forced to leave the only place she knew as home. And who meets Hagar and talks to her? ___________
    - Why do you think He asked her, "Where do you come from and where are your going?" if God knows all?

- Verse 13: How does Hagar respond? Are you surprised?

    - Do you think Hagar knew God?

- Verse 15: Hagar has a son. What name did Abram give him? ____________ (meaning = 'God hears')

Day 3

- Genesis 21: 8 – 21 Hagar and Ishmael sent away…again!
    - It's Isaac's day to be weaned! Sarah spies Ishmael, mocking Isaac's celebration. This does not go over well with Sarah. So, what does she do?

    - Verses 12 – 13: What was God's response to Sarah's request to Abraham? Do you find this surprising? Why, or why not.

        - What promise does God make to Abraham about Ishmael?

- Verses 14 – 16: So, Abraham prepares water and bread, says good bye and sends Hagar on her way. Eventually the water and bread run out. What does Hagar do in this most dreadful moment of her life?

- Picture it: A young, heartbroken mother has just left her son in the shade to die. She has no more means to support him, nor can she see any future for them both. She has been sent away from their home. She fears that if she were to return home, she may lose her son or face more tribulation from another woman. She has nowhere else to turn but to God; this is where Hagar has found herself. Helpless. She was told once by God that Ishmael would be blessed, but she cannot see how that will ever occur without his flesh being feed. God takes this moment to remind Hagar of His promise to her. How about you? Have you ever felt that you were at a crossroad? Are you there now? Just as God reached out to save Hagar and her son, God will do the same for you. All He ask is that we seek Him first (Matthew 6:33).

- Verse 19 – 21: What does God do for Hagar and Ishmael? AMAZING!

Day 4

- Galatians 4: 22 – 31 Paul compares Hagar and Sarah
  - Background: The Galatian people argued with Paul saying there were children of Abraham, and therefore blessed. The Galatian's were children form the lineage of Ishmael. Paul wanted the Galatian's to see the difference from being children of bondage verses children of freedom. He connects

the actions of the flesh (Ishmael's birth) to that of bondage. Whereas, the actions of the spirit (Isaac's birth) to that of freedom.

- Verse 22 – 23: What does Paul mean when he says that one son was born by the flesh, and the other son was born by a 'divine promise'?

- Verse 24 – 27: Paul compares the acts of the flesh (Hagar) verse the acts of the spirit (Sarah) and their linage. Hagar is linked to Mount Sinai in ________________. Sarah is linked to ________________(country). (See Isaiah 54:1)
- Verses 28 – 29: Paul describes the child born of the flesh persecuted by the child born of the spirit. What is Paul referring too?

- Verses 30 – 31: He finishes up his argument with a quote from Genesis 21:10. After reading verses 30 -31, look up Genesis 21:10. Who spoke these words in Genesis, and how are they relevant to Paul's circumstances in Galatian?

Here is a little bit about Hagar...

Hagar was an Egyptian woman and not even a Jew, so what can we learn from her? She was a slave who worked under Sarah's command. Being a slave put her in a position without a voice. She was subject to her owner. Her opinion held no value to Sarah or Abraham. When Sarah asked Abraham to sleep with Hagar, it wasn't out of love. She was forced to be with this man and bear him a child.

I can't even imagine how she felt, pregnant and always under the sharp eye of Sarah. Hagar knew Sarah was barren. She felt the unspoken tension between herself and her boss. As the baby grew inside her, she must have felt love and compassion for her child. Yet what would become of him? Would Sarah force her hand and take the child as her own?

From day one of Ishmael's birth, Hagar knew that they were not wanted by Sarah. Then Sarah forced Abraham to send her and her young son away. Didn't Abraham love Ishmael? After all, he was the father of this forsaken child.

But God had a plan. God opened the eyes of Hagar. How did she learn about God? We do not learn of this in God's Word. Maybe it was from living under Abraham's tent for so long. I am taking a guess on how she became a woman of faith. When God spoke to Hagar, she recognized and listened to His voice. She received His Words, and God helped Hagar see the truth. She and her son dwelt in the wilderness, but she knew God was with them both.

Hagar's life was one of humbleness, confusion, jealousy, and contentment. As a slave, she had no choice but to obey Sarah and Abraham. Her and Sarah's bout with jealousy was felt both ways. Sarah was jealous of Hagar's ability to bear a child, and Hagar was jealous of Abraham's abounding love for Isaac. So, what do we learn from Hagar's life?

1. Hagar was **humble** to her owner.

> Then the angel of the LORD told her, "Go back to your mistress and submit to her." (Genesis 16:9 NIV)

2. Hagar learned that God is **faithful**.

> Then God opened her eyes and she saw a well of water. So she went and filled the skin with water and gave the boy a drink. (Genesis 21:19 NIV)

3. Hagar learned to be **content** in her situation because she knew that **God was with her** in all that she did.

CHAPTER 1 THRU 12 MEMORY VERSES

Rewrite your memory verses from the previous chapters below. I have given you your memory verse for chapter 12. Chose which translation you would prefer to use for this verse. Copy it below! Happy memorizing!

Chapter 1 memory verse:
Chapter 2 memory verse: Hebrews 11:23
Chapter 3 memory verse:
Chapter 4 memory verse: Ruth 1:16

Chapter 5 memory verse:

Chapter 6 memory verse: 2 Corinthians 11:3

Chapter 7 memory verse:

Chapter 8 memory verse: Luke 10: 41 - 42

Chapter 9 memory verse:
Chapter 10 memory verse: Hebrews 11:11
Chapter 11 memory verse:
Chapter 12 memory verse: Genesis 16: 9 - 10

CHAPTER 11 REVIEW

Hagar

1. Did our character this week have a relationship with God? If so, describe that relationship. Include any changes that may have occurred with this relationship.

2. Describe this woman's character. What can we learn from her about faith, love, marriage, being a mother, grief, strength, perseverance, and more.

3. List an example of how this woman handled a specific struggle. Pay attention to details. These details help teach us right steps verses wrong steps to take.

4. What can we learn about being a wife or mother from this woman's story?

Appendix A

Example of Mapping God's Word

2 Corinthians 12:9-10

Write It Down and Map It Out

"But He said to me. 'My grace is sufficient for you, for my power is made perfect in weakness.' Therefore I will boast all the more gladly about my weaknesses, so that Christ's power may rest on me. That is why, for Christ's sake, I delight in weakness, in insults, in hardships, in persecutions, in difficulties. For when I am weak, then I am strong."

Commentary

Greek words for:
Grace = that which affords joy, pleasure, delight, sweetness, charm, loveliness; grace of speech
Sufficient = to be possessed of unfailing strength; to be strong, to suffice, to be enough; to be satisfied; to be content
Weaknesses = want of strength of the body or of the soul
Rest on me = to dwell = to take possession of…house, citizens, power of Christ upon one

(By David Guzik) God was responding to Paul's request. Instead of removing the thorn from Paul's life, God gave and would keep giving His grace to Paul. The grace given was sufficient to meet his needs. God was strengthening Paul under the load he was bearing, and God's strength would be evident in Paul's ability to overcome his own weakness. How was God's grace enough? God's grace met Paul's need because it expresses God's acceptance and pleasure in us. Plus, God's grace was available all the time. Lastly, God's grace could meet Paul's need because it was the very strength of God. Paul was taught all these things through this time of suffering. Paul's response proves his love and trust in God. His endurance is evidence that God's strength can and will help us to endure.

Summary

Thank you God for your grace. You pour down grace upon me, even when I don't deserve it. Just like Paul, Your grace can help me endure the struggles of life. My struggles are nothing compared to Paul's struggles. I want to be more like Paul. I want to have the strength and faith he possessed through you, God.

Apply it to your life

Lord, help me to remember your grace IS sufficient for me. No matter what I face, you are right there beside me through it all. You shower me with grace beyond grace so that I may endure.

Pray it back to God

Lord, I want to use my struggles in life to show evidence of your strength and power. Allow me to keep my eyes on You in all that I do. No matter what trial or struggle I am facing, I want YOU to be the center of it all. I will hide Your Word in my heart; so that I can remind myself to look to you. Thank You Father!

Appendix B

Memorization techniques

Beginning in chapter 1, I encourage each woman to select a verse to memorize. You may choose from the weekly focus verses or select one of your own. These verses are used as building blocks for implementing a closer walk with the Lord. He is our rock that we build our foundation upon. There is never going to be a better time than the present to add to our foundation.

Here is a list of suggestions you may use to help conquer the struggle of memorization. These are methods I have used through the years. One method may work well for one person, while another person needs to try another method.

- Write out your verse on an index card. Read the card over and over—not just in your head but say the words out loud. The next day hand the card to another person. Recite the verse from memory.
  - Highlight, underline, or circle key words. When memorizing, refer to these key words to help you remember the entire verse.
  - Put the reference for the verse on both sides of the card. That way if you need to study alone, you can always look at the side with the reference and then recite the verse.
    - You may find that putting the key words on the side with the reference will also help you memorize the verse.

- The more you write, read, and hear the verse, the easier it will be to memorize it.
    - o Write the verse over and over in your journal or just on scrap paper. This may seem silly, but you may find this is just what gets you through.
- Use a different translation: be careful that you don't lose the true meaning of the verse by watering it down.
- Make flash cards to play memory as you add more and more verses to your list.

About the Author

Let me introduce myself. My husband, Curt, and I have been married for twenty-three years. We have three amazing children; live on a farm with lots of different animals; love our outside dog, Sadie; and spoil our inside dog, Opal. We have a mother-in-law suite attached to our home, where my mother-in-law lives. She has been a major blessing to our home. She helps me keep up with laundry and even does a little cooking from time to time.

I have been a middle school teacher for the past twenty years. I love children, and I love my job. As the years go by, I am saddened by the changes I see in our children and in education. Educational expectations have driven so many children into believing they have no value or worth. With so many dysfunctional families, I have seen a decline in respect given to the teacher by students and parents. My job has become more difficult each year. I continue to remain teaching only because God has not told me it's time to move on. But my heart is becoming heavy.

My husband is a full-time farmer. However, that has not always been his occupation. When Curt and I first me and for the beginning of our marriage, Curt worked in a factory. He made excellent money, usually worked first shift, and was able to keep the job at work. He didn't come home frustrated from the day's activities. It seemed perfect. We had money, time, and lots of love. His father, a full-time farmer, became ill. Curt had to start helping him on the farm after working in the factory all day. We lived about twenty minutes from the farm. We had no children at the time. Adding this extra work to our daily load didn't cause much stress to our lives. I just spent more time with his family and riding in tractors or trucks with my man. Curt's dad continued to decline in health, and Curt had to spend more and more time on the farm. We soon discovered that the twenty-minute drive was too much. We began looking for a house closer to the farm. We also decided that this would be a good time to start having children. This added lots of stress as we began to fight over time and how exactly we would make these changes work in our life. Eventually we moved closer and I became pregnant. Thirteen weeks into my pregnancy, our baby's heartbeat stopped. We were at the doctor's office, so excited to finally see our baby on the ultrasound screen. But our joy quickly turned into sorrow. Our doctor ordered a D and C (dilation and curettage) surgery. I could not remove my child from my body so quickly. So she moved the surgery five days away. Two days after my doctor's appointment, I went into labor. With this being my first pregnancy, I had no idea what was happening. My husband called my best friend, who was a nurse. She and Curt drove me to the hospital, where my OBGYN was called and removed my precious child from my body. This whole experience rates as one of the worst experiences in my life. This experience set a spiral of emotional unbalance for me. Within six months, I was pregnant again. I lived in fear every day, wondering if God would choose to take this child from me too. I had started my job as seventh grade teacher. I used my job to keep me busy—a distraction from my worries. Nine months (and two weeks) later, I delivered my beautiful daughter, Kaytlin. Two years later I had Noah. Two years after Noah, I experienced another miscarriage. This time my baby lived nine weeks in my womb. I knew before the doctors even told me the heartbeat was gone. Just a mother's instinct, I guess. One year later I had my youngest, Caleb. My emotional anxiety remained unbalanced for a large majority of this time in my life. Many stories of my behavior and reactions toward my children are shared in this book. My reactions were many times blown out of proportion, as I tried to understand life through a foggy lens. This is something many women go through, and the best way to handle ourselves during these times is to learn from one another.

Our oldest, Kaytlin, turned nineteen this year. She has started her own business as a photographer. It has been exciting to watch God move in her life. Our middle child, Noah, turned seventeen this year. He helps his dad on the farm. He has also started his own cattle and rabbit business. He has both animals in the barn and spends a majority of his time there. He enjoys anything that is outdoors. Caleb is the youngest and the comedian of the gang. He is thirteen years old with a heart of gold. He will talk to anyone who will listen about anything they'll listen to. He can spin a yarn no matter who, when, or where. His laughter rings through our house daily.

Throughout this book series you are going to learn a lot more about me and my family. I was not always the best mom or wife. I have made mistakes along the way. Hindsight is always twenty-twenty. I pray that my triumphs and failures may be lessons you can learn from.

Endnotes

1 “Denomination”. Meriam-Webster, Incorporated. July 8, 2019. https://www.merriam-webster.com/dictionary/denomination.

2 “Religion” Meriam-Webster, Incorporated. July 8, 2019. https://www.merriam-webster.com/dictionary/religion.

3 “Relationship” Meriam-Webster, Incorporated. July 8, 2019. https://www.merriam-webster.com/dictionary/relationship.

4 “Blue Letter Bible”. https://www.blueletterbible.org/.

Printed in the United States
By Bookmasters